LETTING GO OF DEBT

◆ ◆ ◆

"*Letting Go of Debt: Growing Richer One Day at a Time* is a great resource for people who are grasping for air due to the emotional weight of money struggles. The book gives you the motivation and strength to make it through another debt-free day. As a financial recovery counselor who assists people with difficult money issues, I see many people who will benefit from having this book close at hand."

> —Steve Rhode
> Host of DebtRadio.com
> Author, *Get Out of Debt: Smart Solutions to Your Money Problems*
> President, Debt Counselors of America

"Hazelden has done it again—brief, insightful, and compassionate road map to the land of living debt-free with spiritual calm."

> —Tom Tucker, CCGC
> Executive director, California Council on Problem Gambling

"*Letting Go of Debt* addresses compulsive debting with such a satisfying mix of information and insight that it may well become an essential guide for anyone affected by this addiction. Casanova has a special way of connecting practical decisions made by the afflicted with spiritual growth. Her recommendations continually move the reader closer to surrender and recovery."

> —Mary Heineman, CSW, CGC
> Author, *Losing Your Shirt: Recovery for Compulsive Gamblers and Their Families*

Letting Go of Debt

GROWING RICHER
ONE DAY AT A TIME

❖ ❖ ❖

KAREN CASANOVA

Hazelden
Publishing

Hazelden
Center City, Minnesota 55012-0176

1-800-328-0094
1-651-213-4590 (Fax)
www.hazelden.org

Library of Congress Cataloging-in-Publication Data
Casanova, Karen, 1961–
    Letting go of debt: growing richer one day at a time / Karen
Casanova.
        p. cm.
    Includes index.
    ISBN 978-1-56838-367-5
        1. Finance, Personal. 2. Debt. I. Title.

HG179 .C336 2000
332.024—dc21   00-021180

21   11   10   9   8

Cover design by Mary Brucken
Cover illustration by Mercedes McDonald
Interior design by David Enyeart Design
Typesetting by David Enyeart Design

◆   ◆   ◆

While the author does not endorse any particular money management program, she refers to spending plans and records—basic money management techniques common to various programs—throughout. Definitions of these and other possibly unfamiliar terms are provided below.

Higher Power. A power greater than oneself. The power can be God, the universe, or the feeling generated by a support group. The term is used by people who believe in a God, who do not believe in a God, or who have difficulty visualizing a loving God.

slippery places. Places debtors should avoid because of the likelihood of spending money without regard to financial standing. Compulsive spenders may, for instance, need to stop going to home parties, garage sales, malls, and even grocery stores. Slippery places for gamblers include casinos, racetracks, and bingo parlors.

spending plan. A chart of predicted and actual spending to help plan monthly expenditures. The *spending plan* uses the spending record as its basis. The goal is to ensure that spending does not exceed total monthly net income. If it does, the debtor revises the spending plan accordingly.

spending record. A consistent listing of expenditures that provides a portrait of spending habits and that helps debtors determine the categories in which they can decrease or increase spending. A *daily spending record* includes the exact amount of money spent and what it was spent for (e.g., gas, clothing, food). Daily expenses can be tracked on note cards, in a notebook, or in a daily planner. Daily expenses are summarized in a *weekly spending record.* A weekly spending record lists the categories (e.g., groceries, rent, entertainment), the amount spent in each category each week, and the total amount spent during each week. The *monthly spending record* is a summary of the weekly spending records.

This book is dedicated to my grandfather John,
for showing me the richness of simple abundance.

◆   ◆   ◆

ACKNOWLEDGMENTS

◆ ◆ ◆

I am indebted to a great number of people, past and present.

A special thanks to Dave Kulsrud for his unflagging perseverance in digging up the perfect quotes, for his honest feedback, and for his friendship.

To Sergey for giving me a reason to write this book and for teaching me much about life and myself. To Chas, Kerry, Paul, LeAnn, Dan, Amy, Hector, Mary R., Mary W., and Jean H. for being there. To *everyone* at Hazelden for making such a positive difference in my life. To my "dream" editor, Corrine Casanova, for her skill, positive attitude, sense of humor, patience, and name.

To my children—Mary and Michael—for giving me a reason to get out of debt, for keeping me responsible, and for providing an unending supply of fun and laughter. My mother, Nellie, whose loving, spiritual, and practical self contributes greatly to my well-being and resiliency. To my brother and sister, Jim and Jean, for their generosity and support. And to my deceased father, Albert, for never owning a credit card.

January 1

The significant problems we face cannot be solved at the same level of thinking we were at when we created them.

—ALBERT EINSTEIN

◆　◆　◆

It's easy to live as though our problems will just go away. We say tomorrow, next month, or next year will be better. We keep some kernel of hope that things will change, even though we haven't done anything to change things. Herein lies a paradox. We need to be positive, to let go, and to live one day at a time, but we also need to be sensitive to points in our lives that require us to take action.

Before we can begin to get out of a rut, to make positive change, we need to acknowledge that a problem exists in the first place and that we are responsible for doing something about it. When we can pinpoint the problem, we create a new awareness. We're suddenly open to receiving information we previously blocked out. We reach a higher level of thinking regarding our situation.

Today on this New Year's Day I will admit to myself and another the true source of my financial grief. I will actively seek information about how to help myself or others and will be open to different philosophies.

◆　◆　◆

January 2

You cannot escape the responsibility of tomorrow
by evading it today.

—ABRAHAM LINCOLN

◆ ◆ ◆

Some of us don't feel entirely responsible for our debt. In the back of our minds, we're thinking that the credit card companies gave us the cards in the first place, that our spouse is the reckless one, that everyone has a lot of debt these days, or that our parents never taught us how to manage money.

Regardless of who spent the money or why, we made choices in our life that now leave us in debt. We are responsible for our situation—not creditors, spouses, relatives, or friends. When we accept that the burden is ours, the road ahead may seem long, but we don't waste energy blaming others. As a result, we gain some serenity and can begin to create positive and workable solutions to our situation.

Today I will recall choices I've made that have put me in debt. I will accept that my debt is mine and not blame others for my circumstances.

◆ ◆ ◆

January 3

I may not have gone where I intended to go,
but I think I have ended up where I intended to be.

—Douglas Adams

◆　◆　◆

Throughout the years, various concerns require a great deal of our attention. We focus on diapers and bottles and getting the baby to sleep through the night. We put much of our social life aside while we take evening classes to get a degree. We challenge ourselves and train to climb a mountain. We concentrate on paying off our debt.

What weighs most on our minds these days? When our priorities are in line with goals, we feel good about what we're doing. We're working toward something we want, something that's important to us. We're being proactive. We're taking charge. We're taking responsibility for our well-being.

Today I will write down my top three priorities.

◆　◆　◆

January 4

To keep the body in good health is a duty . . . otherwise
we shall not be able to keep our mind strong and clear.

—BUDDHA

◆ ◆ ◆

Flight attendants instruct adult passengers to place
the oxygen mask on themselves first, before putting
it on children. Given that if we can't breathe we can't
very well help our children, this makes perfect sense.

If we're not in good shape mentally, physically, spiritually, and emotionally, how can we expect to be
healthy and energetic enough to be creative and responsible with our debt? A healthy mind and body also keep
us out of costly clinic or hospital visits. Depending on
our situation, we look at nutrition, exercise, sleep, relationships, quiet time, and entertainment as some possible top priorities. We make paying debt our third or
fourth priority.

Today I will ask myself whether I've made self-care a priority.

◆ ◆ ◆

January 5

The whole world steps aside for the man
who knows where he is going.

—ANONYMOUS

◆　◆　◆

Having priorities can help us make decisions. When
we're not sure whether to go out to dinner with
friends or to get some needed rest, we review our priorities. If our top priority is getting enough rest, our
decision is made. If our top priority is getting out more
often, we again have our answer.

When we write down our priorities (e.g., eating nutritious food, exercising, paying off credit cards, cutting
costs, learning money management, dealing with emotional pain), we experience a paradigm shift. We stop
complaining and start moving forward. We take on the
challenge. We become empowered and incredibly energized by the simple act of consciously moving toward
a goal or at least of knowing what it is we really want.

**Today I will keep my top priorities in mind
when making any decision.**

◆　◆　◆

January 6

Settle for nothing less than what you truly desire,
and do not be afraid to ask for what you feel will
bring you joy and fulfillment.

—EMMANUEL

◆　◆　◆

What are our goals? Have we taken even an hour of our life to look at what it is we'd truly like to be doing or having one, five, or ten years from now? Doesn't it seem odd that we spend incredible amounts of time and energy worrying about tomorrow instead of creating tomorrow?

We look at our priorities, whether self-care, being a better parent, paying off debt, or buying a home. We address each category. If the category is debt, we may decide that a reasonable goal is to be debt-free (free of unsecured debt) within five years. To achieve that goal, we list several action steps. We can read books on money management, attend free workshops, document all expenses, prepare a spending plan, attend Debtors Anonymous or other support group meetings, see a therapist for our addiction, or visit a financial planner. Each of these action steps usually requires mini–action steps, such as looking up numbers in the phone book or finding a sensible way to record expenses.

**Today I will know I can create
my future by planning for it.**

◆　◆　◆

January 7

The way to achieve happiness is to have a high standard
for yourself and a medium one for everyone else.

—MARCELENE COX

◆ ◆ ◆

We have big plans and goals. We feel ready to
move forward, but we're dependent on others.
"If so-and-so would do such and such at this time, I'd
be able to take on some extra work." We expect others
to operate in our framework, on our timelines. We
expect them to understand our needs. We may even
expect them to read our minds!

The level of our expectations is directly related to our
level of serenity. The more we expect of others, the
more disappointed we can get. This is not to say that
we forget our dreams. We still think as big as we'd like,
and we still seek support from others. We just learn that
we can't connect our expectations—our thinking—with
someone else's behavior without running the risk of
being disappointed. We accept that we cannot change
another. We accept reality with grace and move forward
from there.

**Today I release others from my expectations.
In doing so, I gain serenity.**

◆ ◆ ◆

January 8

First we form habits, then they form us. Conquer your
bad habits, or they'll eventually conquer you.

—DR. RON GILBERT

◆ ◆ ◆

We go through stages when we get distracted.
Instead of focusing on our projects at hand, we
find something or someone to complain about and
make it our mission to let everyone know our thoughts.
Our gripes are big and small. The banker is a jerk. The
driver who cut us off on the street has a lot of nerve.
Our doctor doesn't listen.

What comes around goes around. We remove ourselves from situations where we feel tempted to waste
our energy secretly hurting others. We imagine what it
feels like to be the recipient. We ask our Higher Power
for forgiveness and secretly ask those we've harmed for
forgiveness. We make it a habit to act with honor.

**Today I will think good thoughts
and say good things.**

◆ ◆ ◆

January 9

I don't have five dollars to spare for the month.

—STUART B.

◆　◆　◆

If we aren't compulsive spenders (or if we're recovering compulsive spenders), we may be guilty of underspending. Because we're in debt, we become overprotective of family finances. While our spouse is out gambling, we're shopping at garage sales and eating potatoes for lunch. Even though we truly need some new clothes for work, we leave the mall empty-handed, or with something for the kids or a gift for a friend.

When we can't spend money on ourselves, we may have crossed the line from practicality to deprivation. Depriving ourselves means we think we don't deserve to have anything nice or new.

Balance is everything. We examine our priorities. If the purchase is a necessity and a priority, we add it to our spending plan.

Today I will tell myself that I am worthy of giving to myself, and I am worthy of receiving.

◆　◆　◆

January 10

Money talks . . . but all mine ever says is good-bye.
—Anonymous

◆　◆　◆

Our money is spent before the paycheck comes. Every cent is earmarked to pay bills. We wonder how or if we'll make it till the next check comes. We scheme. We rob Peter to pay Paul. It feels futile. We want to treat ourselves, even though we've spent our entertainment money for the month. We say it's Friday and payday; let's go out to dinner or order a pizza. We deserve it.

When we start feeling sorry for ourselves, we challenge our thoughts. We think, think, think—beyond the impulse. We do deserve it, but treating ourselves doesn't have to mean spending money. There are a million ways to treat ourselves without spending a cent.

Today I will, by myself or with another, brainstorm a list of simple treats that rely only on me—a hot bath, a walk in the park, an exercise routine. Treats that will not only reward me but also will improve me.

◆　◆　◆

January 11

Discretion is that honorable stop.
—**WILLIAM SHAKESPEARE**

◆　◆　◆

Newsletters, books, and Internet sites are full of advice on frugality, tips many of us can benefit from. We find tips on everything from how to make homemade Play-Doh to how to pay off a mortgage in seven years. We need to be careful of how "cheap" we become. Moving from spending too much to constantly making sure we're saving every possible cent can be moving from a compulsive behavior to an obsessive one.

When considering all the cheaper options, we select what feels right to us—what works best given our lifestyle. We learn to trust ourselves enough to know what's best. Finding the most appropriate and balanced lifestyle is a matter of trial and error.

Today I will strive for progress, not perfection, in finding the cost-cutting methods that suit me.

◆　◆　◆

January 12

> You've got to create a dream.
> You've got to uphold the dream.
> If you can't, go back to the factory
> or go back to the desk.

—ERIC BURDON

◆　◆　◆

We develop goals, priorities, and action steps. We feel energized and ready to move full speed ahead. But midway, as our momentum picks up, new thoughts enter our mind. *Do I really want this? What if it creates new problems for me? If I reach this goal, I'll have nothing to look forward to.*

Being wishy-washy gets us nowhere. These thoughts are the ego's way of looking for obstacles. We acknowledge the doubts and then quickly cast them aside and move forward with complete conviction, like a warrior. If the goal still feels right, we keep moving ahead. We know in our hearts that doing what we believe in keeps us on the right path.

Today I will believe in my goals.

◆　◆　◆

January 13

If I had my life to live over, I'd try to make more mistakes next time. I would relax. I would limber up. I would be sillier than I have been this trip. I know of very few things that I would take seriously. . . . I would start barefooted earlier in the spring and stay that way later in the fall. I would play hooky more. . . . I would ride on more merry-go-rounds. I'd pick more daisies.

—UNKNOWN

◆　◆　◆

With good reason, we take our debt and the circumstances surrounding it seriously. Thoughts of our debt and what we need to do about it can become a kind of background noise. We adapt to the point where we no longer even hear the hum; it's just a part of our days, forever dulling our senses and demeanor.

We acknowledge that our debt and the circumstances surrounding it are there regardless of whether we wear a smile or a frown. We let ourselves enjoy what comes before us—a sunrise, dew on a flower petal, the warmth of a hug. We forget our troubles long enough to pick some daisies.

Today I will be grateful that life offers more beauty than challenges.

◆　◆　◆

January 14

Honesty is the first chapter of the book of wisdom.

—THOMAS JEFFERSON

❖ ❖ ❖

Some of us deny that our money problems are our own. We want to blame another, bad luck, our health, the economy, or the world. We're the victims. We complain to patient listeners. We look away from the truth.

Honesty is a powerful force. It propels people and relationships forward. Because honesty is real, it is not mistaken for manipulation. Honesty begets respect, self-confidence, and empowerment. By being honest, we let the world know we aren't victims. We acknowledge our power to change. By being comfortable enough to expose our truest and deepest thoughts and feelings, we reveal the admirable qualities of self-confidence and self-esteem. When we're honest, we evolve. In evolution lies the mystery and excitement of life.

Today I will be honest with myself and another about my relationship with money.

❖ ❖ ❖

January 15

To change and to change for the better
are two different things.
—GERMAN PROVERB

◆　◆　◆

Hear the word *budget* and most of us cringe. *Budget* has connotations of scrimping and saving and, worst of all, deprivation. Saving money through a budget can be likened to losing weight on a diet. When we're on a diet, we may deprive ourselves of foods we love, foods that nourish our souls. On a budget, we end up depriving ourselves of basic needs, including a need to be around art or to dine with friends. Most diets and budgets fail.

We choose a spending plan over a budget. With a spending plan, we outline basic needs and see that they are met first, even before we decide how much to pay creditors. We take care of ourselves and our families. We feel abundance.

Today I will write down the names of two or three family members, friends, or members of a support group whom I can ask to help me develop (or revise) a spending plan.

◆　◆　◆

January 16

To live is to change, and to be perfect
is to have changed often.
—JOHN HENRY NEWMAN

◆ ◆ ◆

We spend without knowing where the money went.
The paycheck is gone, but where did it go? A
spending plan is a positive way to look at where our
money is going—to clearly see our spending pattern.
First and foremost, a spending plan recognizes personal
basic needs, from food to a savings account.

Before we get to the point where we create a realistic spending plan, we map out an ideal spending plan.
It has no limits. We go to town and write down what
we'd truly love to be spending money on. We start by
keeping track of income and expenses for six weeks. We
look at how we spend in each category—savings, personal care, baby-sitting, entertainment, medical and
dental care, gifts, vacations, and so on. Are we over-
spending somewhere? Where do we deprive ourselves?
What are our physical, emotional, mental, and spiritual needs?

**Today I will begin to record
my daily expenses and income.**

◆ ◆ ◆

January 17

Go confidently in the direction of your dreams.
Live the life you have imagined.
—HENRY DAVID THOREAU

◆　◆　◆

Following a spending plan makes us solvent. Solvency is the state of being able to pay debts and of being able to pay cash for new expenditures (not necessarily including a car or home). We plan for necessary major and minor purchases. We put money in savings for them, even before paying creditors. We pay cash instead of incurring more unsecured debt.

We feel a great deal of relief. These new spending and saving patterns can make us feel confident. After all, we are able to meet our basic needs, to live our lives, without getting deeper into debt. We may also be afraid—afraid we won't have enough—or we may feel guilty for thinking of ourselves first. We trust that in time confidence will prevail.

Today I will know that solvency based on an honest spending plan will bring tremendous relief.

◆　◆　◆

January 18

It is the greatest mistake of all mistakes to do nothing because you can only do a little. Do what you can.
—SYDNEY SMITH

◆　◆　◆

We commit to a spending plan. We most likely adhere to a payment schedule that we need to maintain for at least a couple of years, and, for those of us buried in bills, for many years to come. We view our payments as a challenge. We may feel some excitement at the thought of making progress. We see, on paper, that it's possible to emerge from the chaos. Then, despair creeps in, overshadowing the promising thoughts. We have doubts. Obviously, adding to our debt doesn't help toward paying it off. How do we discipline ourselves to stick to our spending plan for two, three, five, or seven years—or the rest of our life?

We take it a day at a time. Who knows what will happen tomorrow? Instead of focusing on what we can't have, we concentrate on what we gain—lowered debt, a sense of achievement, integrity, and self-confidence.

Today I will stay committed to my spending plan.

◆　◆　◆

January 19

Half the people in America are faking it.

—ROBERT MITCHUM

◆ ◆ ◆

We have a job where we earn more money than we'd ever dreamed possible, or perhaps we inherited a large sum—or even won the lottery. We always thought if we just made a given amount every year or won a chunk of cash, we'd be okay. We'd be happy. But we find the more we make, the more we spend. And we're still not happy. What happened?

When our appetite is always bigger than our bankroll, we remember to treat the true source of the problem. When by reasonable standards we make plenty of money but our spending and income increase proportionately, we question our thoughts about money, our spending patterns, and our needs: emotional, physical, spiritual, and mental.

Today I will ask myself whether I like being in debt.

◆ ◆ ◆

January 20

We never know how high we are
Till we are called to rise
And then if we are true to plan
Our statures touch the skies.

—EMILY DICKINSON

◆ ◆ ◆

When we first stop using credit cards, we may truly be in some financial binds. We haven't had time to get over the initial hump. We haven't fully implemented our spending plan, and we don't yet have a savings account worth mentioning.

We remember that for each and every credit card scenario, there is an alternative. If we trust ourselves enough, calm ourselves so we're able to think it through, we'll stop reacting with credit and start creating solutions—even before we've reached a point where we have a savings account and a realistic spending plan.

We ask ourselves a few questions: Is the purchase absolutely necessary? Can I put it off? Can I do something less expensive? Can I liquidate an asset? Can I borrow from a friend in exchange for collateral? Can I sell something? Can I withdraw from my savings account?

Today I will make a list of alternatives to credit.

◆ ◆ ◆

January 21

There is the risk you cannot afford to take, and
there is the risk you cannot afford not to take.

—PETER F. DRUCKER

◆ ◆ ◆

One of the first and most obvious ways to pay off debt faster is to look for ways to cut excessive, wasteful, and frivolous spending and to apply that money toward our debt. It can be hard to save hundreds of dollars in one category, but, amazingly, it's easy to save five hundred dollars or more by cutting back on smaller expenses. Could we, for instance, replace the two-dollar cup of gourmet coffee with the stuff we get at work? Can we buy generic brands of medicine? Use vinegar instead of expensive cleaning solutions? Use cheaper shampoos and lotions? Bring our lunch to work every now and then?

Cutting back doesn't have to mean doing without. We experiment. Maybe we get gourmet coffee once a week or once a month instead of every day. We may find that we don't miss it as much as we thought we would and that we feel more gratified saving ten dollars a week. We allow ourselves to be flexible. We put the money we save in an envelope or box. We apply the savings toward our debt.

**Today I will look for small ways to save
five hundred or a thousand dollars a year.**

◆ ◆ ◆

January 22

How do you stop an elephant from charging?
Take away its credit cards.

—UNKNOWN

◆　◆　◆

We may have five or six credit cards, maybe more. We juggle the payments, do balance transfers, try to remember what we owe on each balance, what the percentage rates are for each card, and when payments are due.

Our goal is to get down to one or, if we're compulsive spenders or gamblers, zero credit cards. While we still have a balance due, however, we don't take chances. We cut up all but one (or all) credit cards so we're not tempted to use them and create more debt. We keep the card with the lowest interest rate (or a debit card) for emergencies only. We call the credit card company and ask that our credit limit be lowered.

Today I will clean my wallet.

◆　◆　◆

January 23

Distinction is the consequence, never the object,
of a great mind.
—WASHINGTON ALLSTON

◆ ◆ ◆

There's secured debt and unsecured debt. Secured debt is debt covered by collateral. It includes mortgages and car loans—big ticket items that can be repossessed if we fail to make payments. Unsecured debt is credit card debt, money borrowed from Mom and Dad, and unpaid bills. Unsecured debt is basically any money borrowed in cash or on credit without collateral.

The high price of homes and cars makes it impossible for most of us to pay for them with cash. We make the distinction between unsecured debt and secured debt. Secured debt is, for most of us, unavoidable. We accept secured debt as a living expense (while always living within our means). Since most of us choose to make paying secured debt a priority, it can be the basis of a good credit record.

**Today I will accept that secured debt
is a part of life.**

◆ ◆ ◆

January 24

> What you have become is the price you paid
> to get what you used to want.
>
> —MIGNON MCLAUGHLIN

◆　◆　◆

Most of us are likely to obsess about one thing or another for a period of time, sometimes for days, weeks, or maybe even for years. When in debt, we may obsess about getting what we can't afford, our past spending behaviors, or what we could've had if we hadn't gone so deep into debt.

We question our values. Obsessing about what we want or can't have means we value what money can buy—stuff—more than we value money itself. We're really ignoring money altogether. Instead, we can concentrate on what our money can do. We value its ability to grow, and we appreciate money more than a new computer. We begin to see how money can work for us.

Today I will turn my attention from material goods toward money.

◆　◆　◆

January 25

To not accept all of ourselves creates polarity.
Try to live your life only inhaling for five minutes.

—NIRO ASISTENT

◆　◆　◆

If we take the time, most of us could describe the major characteristics of our personality. We all have good points and some not-so-good points. We may, for instance, be very generous and kindhearted. On the flip side, we endanger family finances through reckless spending.

If our natural tendency is to focus on our defects, we haven't accepted them. We write down our character defects. We read the list over. We acknowledge that, for better or worse, for one reason or another, this is who we are. Once we accept ourselves entirely, we are at the starting gate for making change. We're able to exhale.

**Today I will identify and accept
one of my negative traits.**

◆　◆　◆

January 26

A creditor is worse than a slave-owner;
for the master owns only your person,
but a creditor owns your dignity,
and can command it.

—VICTOR HUGO

❖ ❖ ❖

Just as fast as money multiplies for those who have it and manage it well, it dwindles for those of us in debt. Whether we have bad credit, too much credit, or both, we're penalized. Interest rates are higher. We juggle bills and pay late fees and overdraft fees. We're denied loans and low-interest credit cards. We're hounded by creditors. We have good intentions but feel we only get deeper in debt and can't get out from under it. We feel trapped. We get angry. We try to be creative but find only short-term solutions or rejection.

When we accept that penalties and setbacks are not personal attacks, that they are part of a system we can't control, we no longer waste our energy fighting a losing battle.

**Today I will remember that my value
as a human being is worth more
than all the money in the world.**

❖ ❖ ❖

January 27

Life is not a simple equation, and when it comes to money, we may have a common currency, but each of us has a different emotional currency.

—SUZE ORMAN

◆ ◆ ◆

When we choose to commit to a relationship, we commit emotionally, physically, spiritually, and mentally. Many of us, however, give very little serious thought or discussion to our financial commitment. Either we've decided in our heads how the money is going to be managed, or we just figure everything will work out. We may even feel guilty talking about the money end of the relationship. That would, we believe, be focusing on what's least important.

We think again. Each of us brings our own emotional baggage about money to a relationship. Arguments, resentments, manipulation, and deceit can all stem from misunderstandings and fears about money and equality in a relationship and can undermine the happiness of even the best of soul mates. We take considerable time learning what our partner's "emotional currency" is.

Today I will not assume that I understand the financial relationship I have with my partner.

◆ ◆ ◆

January 28

Anything that is given can be at once taken away. We
have to learn never to expect anything, and when it
comes it's no more than a gift on loan.

—JOHN MCGAHERN

◆　◆　◆

Some of us once found money to be a source of security. We looked at it as a way to solve our problems
and to make our future worry-free. We took great care
to save and to not spend foolishly. Now deep in debt,
we feel insecure, afraid, and bitter. We tried hard not
to get in debt. Regardless, here we are.

We learn to view money as a positive energy. If we
don't cling to the energy, and if we trust that all our
needs will be met, money flows to us when we need it.
We realize that, no matter how rich or poor we are, anything can happen. When we had money, we may have
felt we didn't need to worry about the future. Now that
we're in debt, we no longer need to worry about losing money. In debt, we gain a sense of freedom—freedom from the need to be secure.

**Today I will ask my Higher Power to strengthen
my faith. I will know that the less I seek security,
the more secure I will feel.**

◆　◆　◆

January 29

We grow toward the light, not toward the darkness.
—ASHLEY MONTAGU

❖　❖　❖

Some of us made it a policy not to borrow money. We didn't want to feel indebted to anyone. To us, having money meant freedom. When circumstances—perhaps job loss, divorce, death of a spouse, retirement, medical expenses, or addiction—led us into debt, we felt we lost our freedom to do what we wanted to do, to be where we wanted to be, or to go out and have a good time. Money, instead of being our ticket to adventure, became our prison.

Many of us will eventually escape debtor's prison. In the meantime, we know that freedom can be a state of mind. When we free ourselves of worry, hate, blame, expectations, and look back, we are free to just be.

Today I will look within for a sense of freedom.

❖　❖　❖

January 30

You are in a relationship with money, whether you
think of it in these terms or not. And like the other
relationships in your life, this one needs work
to make it successful.

—SUZE ORMAN

◆　◆　◆

Money, like relationships, is an integral part of life.
One of the first steps to dealing with money problems is to recognize that we have our own unique way
of "being" with money. Some of us may characterize
ourselves as penny-pinchers, compulsive spenders, gamblers, overspenders, underearners, or financial wrecks.

How we look at money, how we act with it, and what
we expect from it determine how we relate to it and,
ultimately, how much we have. If we're not happy in a
personal relationship, we might ask ourselves what we
don't like. From there, we look at *our* behavior. What
can we change? If we're not happy with the way we're
relating to money, if we're uncomfortable with the
amount of debt in our lives, we need to look at changing the way we behave with money.

**Today I will admit that I need to work
on improving my relationship with money.**

◆　◆　◆

January 31

The hardest thing to understand in the world
is the income tax.

—ALBERT EINSTEIN

◆　◆　◆

Many of us fear that we don't know enough about tax laws. Our spouse is good with numbers so we let him handle it. Our spouse makes it clear to us that he knows what he's doing. Everything will be fine.

If we suspect that our spouse or recently divorced spouse may be filing erroneous taxes, we may want to file separately so we are not responsible for back taxes, even if filing separately will cost us more money up front. Tax laws change every year. If we've never done taxes and don't feel confident filling out tax forms, we spend the money to have a professional do the work.

Today I will protect my financial future.

◆　◆　◆

February 1

The Lord is my shepherd; I shall not want.

—PSALM 23

❖ ❖ ❖

Life is a paradox. We're advised to be proactive, not reactive. We're supposed to take charge and to create abundance in our world. Yet we're also told to relax because our Higher Power is in charge.

Following our Higher Power's will does not mean we stop living our own life, or stop taking charge. It means we give ourselves the opportunity to experience what our life is meant to be by listening to our inner voice. We follow our desires but do not obsess about outcomes. We know that if things don't go our way, there's a reason, and something better is just around the corner.

Today I will say the Serenity Prayer:
God, grant me the serenity to accept the things I
cannot change, the courage to change the things I
can, and the wisdom to know the difference.

❖ ❖ ❖

February 2

I've developed a new philosophy . . .
I only dread one day at a time.
—CHARLIE BROWN

◆ ◆ ◆

We sometimes develop rigid expectations of how things should go. We keep waiting and hoping, but nothing changes. We desire something so bad it hurts, but nothing happens. We wonder why even simple goals and dreams aren't being reached. When we believe things need to go a specific way and when they don't go as we'd planned, we miss out on the lighter side of life. We dread getting up, paying bills, or engaging in conflicts with collection agencies, the court system, or our families. Life is either dull and mundane or way too stressful.

We know that if our goal is meant to be, we will achieve it. We keep our goal in mind. But instead of focusing on the way we think things should be, we focus on the uncertainty, the mystery of how we're going to get to our goal, or maybe even something better. Knowing everything makes life overly familiar and predictable. We open ourselves up to all possibilities and seize the opportunities as they come. Life takes on an excitement. Life starts to happen.

**Today I will smile when I think of
the uncertainty that lies ahead.**

◆ ◆ ◆

February 3

Just relax. God's in charge.

—ALCOHOLICS ANONYMOUS SLOGAN

◆ ◆ ◆

Sometimes we want something so bad we spend all our time and energy calculating how to get it. We decide that the current state of affairs is unjust and that we know how things *should* be. Our former spouse *should* pay child support. We *should* be able to get our position back after taking a medical leave. We *should* be paid more money. We *should* qualify for that loan. These are reasonable requests. Yet no matter how hard and how long we try to fulfill them, we may end up right back where we started, feeling the same grief and anger.

If our attempts to get what we want fail over and over again, we may be trying to fit a square peg into a round hole. We need goals, ambition, and faith, but we also need to know when to surrender.

We consider whether our objective feels right. If so, we keep it, but we don't sweat the details. We let go and let our Higher Power take over. Maybe there's a better plan in store for us. We don't give up; we give in.

Today I leave myself open to all possibilities.

◆ ◆ ◆

February 4

The power of man has grown in every sphere,
except over himself.
—WINSTON CHURCHILL

◆ ◆ ◆

Some of us who find ourselves deep in debt had always looked at borrowing money as a good investment. We could get ahead in life or build up our business. We liked the feeling of power it gave us. We liked feeling in charge by spending, investing, or borrowing. We took action; we took risks. When circumstances led us deep into debt, we may have denied that money was an issue and told ourselves everything would work out.

Deep down we know that money is only a symbol of power. We choose instead to trust that true power comes from within.

Today I will imagine a life of complete poverty and feel my inner strength and power.

◆ ◆ ◆

February 5

The world needs more warm hearts
and fewer hot heads.

—UNKNOWN

◆　◆　◆

Some days we can't believe how much our relatives and friends don't understand. They criticize our lifestyle, judge our actions, and angrily remind us that they can't take a vacation because they lent their extra cash to us. The temptation is to be defensive, to argue. Can't they see that we're doing the best we can? Can't they look for the positive rather than the negative? Commenting on their attitude only makes matters worse.

We resign ourselves to the fact that it's not our place to convince people that they are critical or judgmental. Lest we act the same, we resist the urge to combat their statements. We know we're doing all we can to stop debting. Instead of starting an argument, we gracefully accept that their feelings are their own. We respond only with loving thoughts that foster a cycle of love and forgiveness.

Whenever I confront negativity about my behavior or situation, I will act with grace.

◆　◆　◆

February 6

Humility invites learning.
—ANONYMOUS

◆　◆　◆

If we're gamblers or compulsive spenders in recovery, we've committed to paying back what we've borrowed or stolen, whether from a friend, a credit card company, or a loan shark. Some of us have debt that will outlive us, but we commit to sending a monthly sum. We're strongly advised to avoid bankruptcy, the "easy" out that doesn't allow us to feel the consequences of our actions.

In paying those we owe, we're reminded of, and continually humbled by, the damage we've done. We take the responsibility of treating money with respect. We stop abusing our relationship with money.

Today I will allow myself to feel humbled by the amount of debt I'm responsible for.

◆　◆　◆

February 7

Opportunities are usually disguised as hard work,
so most people don't recognize them.
—ANN LANDERS

◆　◆　◆

We're told that we can't have the highs in life without experiencing the lows. The degree of joy we feel, for instance, is relative to the degree of pain we've felt. This concept may also be true for the amount of money we make. We've heard stories of entrepreneurs and musicians who were born dirt poor and died filthy rich.

We know that the depth of our experiences determines at times how full our lives are. We trust that being deep in debt is our opportunity, our turning point, the place from which we can find wealth.

**Today I will find hope in knowing
that life is lived in seasons.**

◆　◆　◆

February 8

There is a place at times for debt in all our lives,
but the debt, if it is to be worthy debt, must be
in alignment with the other goals in your life.

—SUZE ORMAN

◆　◆　◆

There's necessary debt, and there's unnecessary
debt. It's important to recognize the differences.
"Good" debt includes money borrowed to help us
achieve the goals we've outlined as being important to
us. This may include a student loan or a mortgage.
Good debt also includes borrowing when we have no
reasonable choice, such as to pay mounting medical
bills. Good debt is often synonymous with secured
debt.

Unnecessary debt is debt we mindlessly (that is, with
no thought of long-term consequences) borrow to buy
clothes, dinners, entertainment, and possessions. We
forgive ourselves for our past behavior regarding unnecessary debt. We recognize what's unnecessary today.

Today I will keep my priorities in mind.

◆　◆　◆

February 9

The tragedy is not when you fool others,
it is when you fool yourself.

—DAVE KULSRUD

◆ ◆ ◆

Each of us brings our own personal bias to our debt. Asking for an advance on our paycheck is not really debt, we say. We'll be at work the rest of the week, so we're earning the money. How about when we borrow five dollars from a friend for lunch? Fall behind a month in our rent to cover other expenses? Pay a bill or two late? Write a check knowing the money isn't in the account—yet?

All of the above is debt. All of the above is debting. We look at our behavior. We listen to our thoughts. We accept that by blowing off responsibilities and putting various labels on our actions; we're talking ourselves into debt. We're manipulating ourselves!

Today I will see debt for what it is.

◆ ◆ ◆

February 10

Do or do not. There is no try.

—YODA

◆ ◆ ◆

Changing our behavior to improve our financial situation is work. We need to check ourselves regularly to make sure we live by our new principles, which are all too easy to forget.

We make ourselves a daily checklist. We start by asking some simple questions: (1) Did I record all my expenditures? (2) Am I following my spending plan? (3) Did I buy something unexpectedly? (4) Have I volunteered any services lately? (5) Is my savings account adequate? (6) Have I created new debt? (7) Am I in touch with members of my support group? (8) Am I valuing relationships more than money?

Today I will create a personalized checklist to track my behavior regarding money.

◆ ◆ ◆

February 11

> The great corrupter of public man is the ego. . . .
> Looking at the mirror distracts one's attention
> from the problem.
> —DEAN ACHESON

◆　◆　◆

We feel a certain comfort with being in debt. After all, it's what we know. It's familiar. We may have opportunities to pay off some debt, yet we don't. We get a bonus, a raise, or a higher-paying job, but the money seems to disappear. Somehow we don't even notice the increase. Vagueness and confusion cloud our money thoughts, and we don't progress.

We ask ourselves some probing questions about how we feel about being in debt. Do we like being in debt? Is it somehow our way of rebelling against the material world and what it stands for? Is being in debt our way of showing the world we're not perfect? Are we trying to be more by spending more? Do our egos stand in the way of progress? If so, why?

Today I will visualize a life without debt and notice any uncomfortable feelings.

◆　◆　◆

February 12

Enablers are the worst enemies of
the very people they love the most.
—EARNIE LARSEN AND
CAROL LARSEN HEGARTY

◆　◆　◆

Bailing someone out is when we give an addict the means to continue an addiction. The addicts play on our love and compassion for them; they know we care. We can give them money, but we can be sure they'll be back again, looking for yet another bailout.

If we're in debt because our spouse, partner, child, parent, sibling, or friend is a gambler, sex addict, drug addict, alcoholic, or compulsive spender, we need to be especially strong and aware. We need to be wise enough to set some unbendable ground rules around money, and we need to be tough enough to stick to them. Refusing to bail out addicts brings them closer to rock bottom. We let go and allow the addict to move forward, toward recovery.

Today I will know that I can't change the addict's behavior, but I can change mine.

◆　◆　◆

February 13

The love of money is the root of all evil.
—1 TIMOTHY 6:10

❖ ❖ ❖

This well-known passage from the Bible is often mis-quoted as "Money is the root of all evil." Money is not the problem. Money is a means to an end. It's neither good nor bad. What's "evil" is when we covet money, when it becomes part of our self-esteem, and when we can't control ourselves with it. Other aspects of our lives—particularly relationships—suffer. Loving money doesn't spread love and joy. It creates frustration, resentment, and anger. If we have it, we may get greedy. If we don't have it, we may get frustrated.

We remember that we need money and that it's okay to have money, but we know that money is not the center of the universe. We consider our values. We imagine what it would be like to be completely broke and compare it with what it would be like to be completely alone, without a friend or family. We feel the difference.

Today I give my love to people—openly to the people who count in my life and silently to strangers.

❖ ❖ ❖

February 14

Life becomes religious whenever we make it so: when
some new light is seen, when some deeper appreciation
is felt, when some larger outlook is gained, when some
nobler purpose is formed, when some task is well done.

—SOPHIA BLANCHE LYON FAHS

◆　◆　◆

It's amazing how our lives can become so settled or
so chaotic that we fail to appreciate the beauty of
what we have. We may, for instance, have been with
the same partner for years and go weeks without having a lengthy or deep conversation. We may have had
the same job for years and never bothered to know our
co-workers better. We may have lived in the same
house for years and never visited the parks or intro-
duced ourselves to our neighbors.

We imagine ourselves with one day or one week left
to live our life as we know it. That's it. What would we
do? What would we say? How would we feel about our
money problems? Would we share how we feel? Why
did we move to the neighborhood in the first place?
What did we see in our partner that we've forgotten
about? We feel the intensity of our deep-seated need
for intimate relationships and simple experiences. We
place relationships above money.

**Today, on Valentine's Day, I will make myself
vulnerable by being honest with one person.**

◆　◆　◆

February 15

Anger is a thief who steals away nice moments.
—JOAN LUNDEN

◆　◆　◆

Being angry with ourselves or another for the debt we're in keeps us stuck. We don't notice how trapped we are unless we experience the opposite—love and forgiveness. When we've truly forgiven, we become free of our anger.

On a tough day, it's easy to slip into our old patterns of blaming and feeling angry. We remind ourselves that great things happen when we are motivated and supported by the force of love.

Today, with an open heart, I will think only good thoughts for and about myself and all others.

◆　◆　◆

February 16

As faith is the evidence of things not seen,
so things that are seen are the perfection of faith.

—ARTHUR WARWICK

◆ ◆ ◆

In some circles, it feels taboo to use the word *God*. In other circles, we cower to think of using the term *Higher Power*. Neither term can appear in public school textbooks. How do we communicate what we believe without feeling that we're offending one group or another?

To many (but certainly not all), the term *Higher Power* seems to communicate spirituality, whereas *God* is linked to religion. Since we don't need to be religious to be spiritual, yet we can be religious and spiritual at the same time, the term *Higher Power* encompasses a larger audience. Many people choose to be all-inclusive by referring to their source as a Higher Power. Referring to our source of love, power, and guidance as a Higher Power doesn't necessarily mean we don't believe in God. *Higher Power* could be the equivalent of *God.* It could be a God within a religion, or it could be a Power Greater that attaches itself to all or no religions.

Today I will trust that my faith itself is far more important than how I define it to others.

◆ ◆ ◆

February 17

This above all: To thine own self be true.

—WILLIAM SHAKESPEARE

◆   ◆   ◆

Maybe our homes are filled with beautiful furniture, fine china, artwork, big-screen TVs, and the latest computer. We have closets bulging with the trendiest fashions, and we have a vast array of shoes and jewelry. We like what we see, but for some reason we don't like what we feel. We may not think our bad feelings have anything to do with our possessions, but when we look closely, we realize we're living a lie. What we show is just that—show. It's not really ours: *we can't afford it!* We're lying to ourselves and to the rest of the world.

When we live a lie we carry a huge burden. We're so used to buying on credit, to having the burden, to living the lie, that we may not even be able to discern the feeling.

Today I will shed some burden by admitting to myself and one other person that I cannot afford what I've purchased on credit.

◆   ◆   ◆

February 18

Equality is giving others the same
chances and rights as myself.

—WALT WHITMAN

◆　◆　◆

We may habitually pay fees a week or two late to
the patient and understanding day-care provider.
We may owe a co-worker five dollars, money we borrowed for lunch a couple of months ago. Did we forget to cover our half of the golf fee our neighbor
picked up? Have we paid the establishment down the
street for the window our son broke? How about the
three thousand dollars we borrowed from our sister?
Do we have a plan to pay her back?

Unrecorded debt usually doesn't accrue interest. It's
just kind of "out there." People we owe don't usually
bring it up; either they don't want to be rude, or
they've forgotten about it. Whether unsecured or
unrecorded, debt is debt. We need to respect that
friends and family deserve to be paid back. We stop
treating unrecorded debt as if it doesn't matter. We pay
our bills in a timely manner. We feel some relief.

Today I will treat all debt equally.

◆　◆　◆

February 19

Life is what happens when
you're busy making other plans.

—JOHN LENNON

◆ ◆ ◆

When our days and nights are clouded by debt, we're in a state of terminal vagueness. We don't know what's coming or going. Our life, in a sense, is passing us by. We're not really participating in it. We're only reacting. That's all we have the wherewithal to do.

These days filled with stress and doubt are the days of our life, as well. The more we experience them, the more we'll learn from them, and the more quickly we'll get to the good times.

Today I will get grounded so that I can be proactive.

◆ ◆ ◆

February 20

When our actions do not, our fears do make us traitors.
—WILLIAM SHAKESPEARE

◆　◆　◆

Some of us live our lives fearing we'll never have enough. As a result, we don't spend money on anything we don't absolutely need for minimal survival. The thought of parting with our money even for small pleasures scares us; it's painful. If someone gave us a big chunk of cash that we could only spend on ourselves, we wouldn't know what to do. We've forgotten what we enjoy. We've forgotten how to take care of ourselves. The result is that we feel deprived and impoverished.

We see ourselves as responsible—overly, perhaps—and conscientious. We think we're doing the right thing. In reality, we're blocking the flow of money to ourselves. We don't give, and we don't get. Actions based on fear are not from the heart. They come from the ego, a place of mixed emotions and uncertainty. To make the right choices for ourselves, we need to listen to that still, small voice within. Fear has a way of drowning out that voice.

**Today I will remember one joy or dream
I had in my youth and will find a way
to reintroduce it into my life.**

◆　◆　◆

February 21

Perception is strong and sight weak.
In strategy it is important to see distant things
as if they were close and to take a distanced view
of close things.

—MIYAMOTO MUSASHI

◆　◆　◆

Some of us deprive ourselves as a discipline. We decide not to eat between meals, or we won't take our vacation until we've saved up the cash for it. Some of us deprive ourselves because we've been in debt for so long we've forgotten how to take care of ourselves. We go months without allowing ourselves a night out, we don't spend money on nutritious food, and we wear sweaters that are ten years old. We think we're being frugal. In truth, we're missing out on some of life's simple pleasures.

There's a fine line between discipline and deprivation. When we can't spend money on ourselves, when we instead spend our lives obsessing over what not to buy, life passes us by. We strive to find the balance that's right for us. We may not need to go out every week or have a closet full of new sweaters. We do, however, need to recognize when we've forgotten how to feel joy and pleasure from what our money can buy.

Today I will look for balance.

◆　◆　◆

February 22

A hobby puts to work those unused talents which might otherwise become restless, and it provides us with a form of activity in which there is no need whatever to strive for success.

—HAL FALVEY

◆　◆　◆

We'd been spending, gambling, drinking, or drugging for years. We spent a great deal of our time in malls, casinos, bars, and on street corners. We spent even more time figuring out how we were going to find the money to sustain our addiction. Addiction takes a lot of time. When we find the strength and courage to give it up, we need to discover ways to fill up our newly found spare time.

We get creative. We recall past interests. We think of what activities we're drawn to now. We keep a list of friends and support group people. We write down fifty things we can do instead of returning to our old behaviors. At first, these new activities may seem boring to us. We give them a try. We fill up our time with new, positive activities.

**Today I will know that in time
I'll appreciate my new life.**

◆　◆　◆

February 23

Every action generates a force of energy that returns
to us in like kind. . . . What we sow is what we reap.
And when we choose actions that bring happiness and
success to others, the fruit of our karma is happiness
and success. . . . The Law of Karma says no debt
in the universe ever goes unpaid.

—DEEPAK CHOPRA

◆　◆　◆

We reap what we sow. If we've been sowing seeds
of hatred and deceit, we can plan on reaping
some of the same. Karmic debt is the equivalent of paying for what we've thought and for what we've done.

We make conscious choices about how we react to
situations and about how we treat people. We choose
to behave as we would like others to behave toward us.

Today I will treat everyone with dignity and respect.

◆　◆　◆

February 24

[The ego] demands our attention and keeps us focusing on what is wrong. In reality, the ego does not protect us— it controls us, unless we learn how to put it in its place.

—WARREN BERLAND

◆　◆　◆

When we think of someone as being egocentric, we think of someone who only looks out for number one. In truth, the stronger our ego, the less we're tending to our real needs. The ego is a part of the personality we create as we go through life. We create it to protect ourselves from being too vulnerable, but if we give it too much power, it ends up controlling us.

How many times have we made up our minds to do something only to talk ourselves out of it? We're too old, too tired, too stupid, or too ugly. That's the ego talking. It's trying to keep its power over us. It doesn't want our true selves—our spiritual selves—to surface, because when that happens, the ego loses and we have to face our fears and doubts.

Discipline is one way to quiet the ego. We assign ourselves small disciplines and practice them daily, regardless of what our ego says about them. In doing so, we quiet the ego and can begin to hear the still, small voice within.

Today I will pick one discipline to practice
every day, whether it be to make my bed,
to walk four miles, or to record my expenses.

◆　◆　◆

February 25

Try not to become a man of success
but rather a man of value.

—ALBERT EINSTEIN

◆ ◆ ◆

Some of us are so entrenched in debt or an addiction that we've forgotten our dreams. We've focused mostly on our problems and given very little thought to how we truly want to live our life. We wake up one day and realize that we have no goals (except to get out of debt), no ideal vision of the future, nothing to work toward.

To realize our dreams, we start with our values. Values are the qualities we respect and honor the most—personal attributes we'd like to develop. They include self-care, healthy relationships, discipline, honesty, professionalism, and even financial independence. When we live according to our values, we feel good about ourselves, and we can make dreams happen.

Determining what values are most important to us allows us to begin to create the life we want. We get a better understanding of what goals would help us uphold those values. Our values become the foundation for our goals—our dreams.

**Today I will list my values
and rank them in importance.**

◆ ◆ ◆

February 26

Let every man sing his own song in life.
—JOHN A. WIDTSOE

◆ ◆ ◆

Mission statements are popular in corporations and even families. We can use them in our selves, too. A mission statement is a paragraph that captures how we want to live our lives. It reflects our values, philosophy, and the overall contributions we'd like to make during our lifetime. Personal mission statements remind us of what's most important to us; they keep us on a positive track so that we can reach our goals.

Personal mission statements need to be well thought out. We need to capture in just a few sentences what's most important to us. We consider what it is we'd most like to *have* (financial independence, healthy relationships), *do* (travel around the world, volunteer at a food pantry), and *be* (generous, truthful, debt-free).

Today, when contemplating my personal mission statement, I will think about what I'd like to be remembered for when I die.

◆ ◆ ◆

February 27

Goals are dreams with deadlines.
—FRANKLIN-COVEY PLANNER

❖   ❖   ❖

We can dream all we want, but to create the life we want, it doesn't hurt to have some goals. Goals can lead us to our dreams. The simple act of writing down a goal and some action steps can make it real. We start to believe in it. As we complete some of the action steps, we affirm that it's possible. We're encouraged to keep working toward our goals.

We determine some goals by reviewing our values. We come up with at least one goal for each value. If one of our values is financial independence, one of our long-range goals would be to liquidate our debt. We then list in order the steps we need to take to reach those goals. We give ourselves deadlines. We record our action steps and deadlines on a calendar or in a planner. We take action.

Today I will write down at least three goals.

❖   ❖   ❖

February 28

The real voyage of discovery consists not in
seeking new landscapes but in having new eyes.

—MARCEL PROUST

◆　◆　◆

Some days we just want to escape from all our struggles. We want to run. We imagine life in a different
location and see our troubles disappear. Everything will
improve, we start to think, if we can just move across
the country.

The notion of the "geographical cure" may pop up
when we feel we don't belong. We want so desperately
to be recognized for our contributions. Each of us
needs to feel we count. If we feel we've failed our present "community," if everyone seems to be down on us
or if people aren't responding to us, we get the urge to
move on.

If we have a history of moving on when things get
tough, we question what we're running from. We can
cross the oceans, but we cannot get away from ourselves. We recognize that it's not the people or the environment we're running from; it's the feelings we don't
want to feel. While we can change the faces and scenery
over and over again, we will not change until we face
our issues.

Today I trust that I belong.

◆　◆　◆

February 29

Even if you're on the right track,
you'll get run over if you just sit there.

—WILL ROGERS

◆　◆　◆

With every opportunity comes responsibility. How we *respond* to the opportunity—whether we are responsible or not—determines the consequences. We may be on the right track. We may know with conviction that we want to get out of debt. But if our response is not to do anything about it—if we just sit on the track—the consequences are increased debt and lowered self-esteem.

When our discretionary income rises because we get a raise or no longer need to pay child support, we respond by consciously directing that money toward our debt. If we have a problem with compulsive spending or gambling, we respond by seeking help for our addiction. If we just need money management skills, we respond by taking classes or reading books and applying what we've learned. We make the effort.

Today I will stay aware of how I choose
to respond to the day's opportunities.

◆　◆　◆

LEADER

March 1

Be bold—and mighty forces will come to your aid.

—BASIL KING

◆ ◆ ◆

Some of us have been in charge of paying bills for a long time. Some of us have never taken on that charge. We've always had someone else to do it for us and our family. Illness, death, divorce, or addiction are all reasons we can suddenly find ourselves in a financial leadership role, directing what happens to the family's money for the first time, or for the first time in a long time. This can be frightening. How will we know what's coming in and when? How do we find out how much money we already have? How do we feel confident we'll make it through the month? Do we need to prepare a budget? Balance a checkbook?

Everyone needs to lead now and then. That's how we discover talents, faults, and truths. It's scary but thrilling, exhausting yet invigorating. We take it one step at a time. We make mistakes. We learn.

Today I will see myself as a leader.

◆ ◆ ◆

March 2

Accept that all of us can be hurt, that all
of us can—and surely will at times—fail.

—DR. JOYCE BROTHERS

◆　◆　◆

If we're going through treatment for compulsive
spending, gambling, or an alcohol or drug addiction,
our families may be forced (or advised) to take over
family finances at least temporarily, if not permanently.
If we've always been in charge of finances, having to
receive an allowance can make us feel powerless and
resentful.

We accept that part of proving we're responsible is
accepting that the money is better off in someone else's
hands for now. We take the necessary time to adapt to
our new relationship with money. We enjoy the freedom that comes with no longer needing to hide our debt
and our spending habits. We use that time and energy
to relax, to heal.

Today I will see myself as a follower.

◆　◆　◆

March 3

The biggest liar was my own addiction.
—JOANIE R.

◆ ◆ ◆

We've been playing the same lottery numbers every week; we can't stop now because we'd never forgive ourselves if the numbers came up after we quit playing. And wouldn't that be our luck! We win a few dollars here and there but know that our chances of winning the lottery jackpot are slim. Yet we cling to the belief that we might just get lucky. We feel lucky enough to win "someday," but feel unlucky about quitting our play. If we quit, our numbers will come up; if we play and don't win, at least we still have a chance.

Our logic around lotteries is some of our best thinking, and our best thinking has gotten us into a great deal of debt. We need to change our thinking. We stop buying tickets; we stop looking up lottery results in the paper; we walk away when they appear on the TV screen. We soon forget what our numbers were.

Today I will question whether the lottery is more of a mind game than a money game.

◆ ◆ ◆

March 4

They are good, they are bad,
They are weak, they are strong,
They are wise, they are foolish—so am I.

—SAM WALTER FOSS

◆　◆　◆

We leave the casino, again, with the same guilt, shame, and emptiness. We take another trip we can't afford or hadn't included in our spending plan. We hang our new clothes in our overstuffed closet. Although we may have enjoyed the experiences, we return worried and upset for spending or losing so much more than we have. We hold on to the same thought pattern and take the same actions, yet we somehow expect different results. We have some strange kernel of hope that things will be different this time.

We can become aware of our patterns. We grow to identify them in their earliest stages. We acknowledge that we know what's going to happen if we repeat the pattern. We do something different—maybe the opposite. We ask our Higher Power for guidance.

Today, when I catch myself wanting to follow through on an unhealthy spending pattern, I will consider doing the opposite of what I normally do.

◆　◆　◆

March 5

Attachment is the great fabricator of illusion;
reality can only be attained by someone who is
detached.

—SIMONE WEIL

◆ ◆ ◆

Detaching, or letting go, is a way of allowing the will of our Higher Power to flow through our lives. When we have a desire, we direct our attention to it. We pray and meditate, releasing our intention, and then we relax and enjoy our days. We accept that things right now are as they should be. We detach, knowing that our Higher Power is taking care of business.

With this assurance, we know we are not creating more problems for ourselves and others. For our Higher Power to get its job done, we detach ourselves from any rigid interpretation of the outcome. We remain open to experiencing whatever comes our way. If the outcome is not as we desired, we know that's okay. We know that our Higher Power has even better plans in store for us. We remain open to the uncertainty. We find comfort and joy in the uncertainty.

Today I will stop writing final scripts
for my various dreams. I will work only from
a rough draft, a version open to change.

◆ ◆ ◆

March 6

True belief transcends itself; it is a belief in
something—in a truth which is not determined
by faith, but which . . . determines faith.

—ERICH FRANK

◆　◆　◆

We pray for our spouse to stop gambling, spending, or drinking and see only temporary results.
We pray for a happy marriage, only to find ourselves
arguing almost daily. What's going on, we say? Where's
our Higher Power when we need it? Why isn't it listening and responding?

Our Higher Power seeks to teach and show us the
truth. Loving parents would not tolerate letting their
toddler play in the middle of the freeway just because
he wanted to. They would bring him home kicking and
screaming because they know it's better for him to be
unhappy in the safety of his backyard than it is for him
to play happily in the middle of a dangerous freeway.

A loving Higher Power takes the same logic. It's not
going to worry whether we're okay with our situation.
It knows we have the means to be happy within. It's not
going to feel responsible for our feelings. Our Higher
Power tries to teach us truths. Rejecting those truths
causes additional, unnecessary suffering.

**Today, rather than blame my Higher Power
for not being there, I will seek the truth.**

◆　◆　◆

March 7

Change is the only thing that has brought progress.
—CHARLES F. KETTERING

◆ ◆ ◆

Some people manipulate, blame, judge, criticize, and betray us. Sometimes this abuse is obvious; sometimes it's well disguised. These types of people are literally toxic to our system. The resulting stress causes physical reactions that are harmful to our bodies, giving us colds, flus, ulcers, stomach pains, cancers, or heart attacks. Emotionally, we feel as if we can no longer function. We numb our feelings. We retreat and isolate to survive. To make matters worse, the people we're most negatively affected by may be the very people from whom we expect love and support: spouses, parents, siblings, and children.

We return to taking care of ourselves. We clearly, honestly, and directly let the toxins in our life know how their behavior makes us feel. If they are unwilling to change, we change. We change how we react. We seriously consider terminating the relationship. In their absence, over time, we feel a great sense of freedom and relief.

Today I will trust that by staying away from toxic people, I will have the freedom to be who I really am.

◆ ◆ ◆

March 8

Compassion for myself is the
most powerful healer of them all.

—THEODORE ISAAC RUBIN

◆　◆　◆

How do we get ourselves to respond to our debt-ing challenges? How do we get spouses to respond to our financial needs? How do we get different results? We can kick ourselves. We can scream and yell at our spouses. We'll get responses all right, but most likely not the ones we need.

It may be safe to say that *everyone* responds to honor and respect and, in many cases, generosity. When we honor and respect ourselves and treat ourselves well, we put ourselves in the best frame of mind for change. We feel confident and capable. The same holds true for others. When we give honor and respect (with detachment) and when we're generous, we create warmth and safety for others. We help to put them in the best place to change.

Today I will try compassion.

◆　◆　◆

March 9

These next twenty-four hours will be unlike
all others. And we are not the persons we were,
even as recently as yesterday.

—KAREN CASEY

◆　◆　◆

We know the routine, and we go through the motions. We rush here and there, barely conscious of what we're doing. In our thoughtlessness, we miss the mystery each new day offers.

We learn to expect the unexpected. Although we think we know how the day will go (routinely), none of us really does. Anything can happen. A minute—a second—can make a difference in our lives, sometimes big and sometimes small. Like a script whose every dialog needs to move the story forward, every day is an opportunity for growth and surprise.

Today I will expect a miracle.

◆　◆　◆

March 10

The hardest thing in life is to know which bridge to
cross and which to burn.
—DAVID RUSSELL

◆　◆　◆

When we're practicing new behaviors, we're step-
ping into unfamiliar territory. We're not always
sure of our next step or comfortable playing a different role. Trying to make decisions can be stressful.
Attempting to face new challenges can be downright
frightful.

We look ahead. If we buy the duplex we're renting,
we may see ourselves looking and feeling like people
in charge of our lives, like people who have their best
interests in mind, like people who are moving forward.
If we continue to rent, we may envision ourselves
moaning and groaning that we can't afford a house,
looking and feeling hopeless and stuck.

Today, when I have a hard time making a decision
or fear taking on new challenges, I will consider
whether I'm working toward the future I want.

◆　◆　◆

March 11

Where we love is home.
—OLIVER WENDELL HOLMES

◆　◆　◆

If we're in a transitory stage in our lives, we may not be sure where we want to hang our hat. Our employer may have transferred us to a new town, we may have just gotten divorced, or we may be experiencing small-town or city living for the first time. We may not want, or be able, to maintain a property, so we choose to rent.

Renting makes sense for many of us. If we intend, however, to live someplace for at least five years, we may want to consider buying a house, townhouse, or condominium—a home more than a place to live; it's an investment. If we're a first-time buyer, a single parent, or fall below a certain income level, we may qualify for a number of federal and state mortgage programs that make owning a home possible.

Today I will weigh the benefits of renting versus owning and will find out what types of mortgage programs I qualify for.

◆　◆　◆

March 12

Real knowledge is to know
the extent of one's ignorance.
—CONFUCIUS

◆　◆　◆

If we're at a point where we're considering separation or divorce, we need to try to keep our intense emotions at bay long enough to make some smart decisions about our financial future. States have different laws regarding separation and divorce. We may, for instance, still be responsible for debt incurred by our spouse during separation, in which case we may want to speed up the process.

The laws are many and varied. Before leaving the house or signing divorce papers, we need to check with a lawyer or accountant to find out what applies to our case. We need to be aware of what we're doing to ourselves financially.

Today I will know that it's important to think about my financial future, especially when in emotional turmoil.

◆　◆　◆

March 13

Advice is like snow—the softer it falls, the longer it dwells upon, and the deeper it sinks into the mind.

—SAMUEL TAYLOR COLERIDGE

❖ ❖ ❖

When we're in the midst of a divorce, we may say we don't care what happens. We just want to get out of the relationship—now. We may even be scared for our safety, fearing that if we ask for anything or don't follow our spouse's "instructions" we'll be in physical danger, or that our spouse will drag out the court proceedings, leaving us even more penniless. Or, in contrast, we may want to use the divorce to get back at our spouse—to "take them to the cleaners."

We need to choose our battles, keeping safety in mind first. If the situation is intense, we'll probably experience fear, anger, or confusion. We need to know what's important at the moment, yet keep an eye on the future. We need to make decisions that are fair and in our best interests. We need to be wise enough to know that we benefit by talking to friends and professionals (therapists, lawyers, accountants) before going to battle in court.

Today I will be open to support and advice.

❖ ❖ ❖

March 14

Teach me, my God and King,
In all things thee to see,
And what I do in anything,
To do it as for thee.

—GEORGE HERBERT

◆ ◆ ◆

Some of us have gone through life unconsciously expecting others to bring us happiness, to make our dreams come true, and to make us feel good about ourselves. When nothing seems to be going well for us, we blame it on the lack of external support—we're not in a serious relationship, we don't like our job, we don't have the money to venture into our own business.

When we change our perspective—when we know and trust that we are responsible for our happiness, our dreams, and our feelings—we become empowered. No longer is the burden on someone or something that is either unreliable or nonexistent. We'd been giving this power to others; now it's time to take it back, to make and be responsible for our own choices, to value our opinions, and to respect our intellect.

**Today I will give myself credit for all
I am capable of, financially and otherwise.**

◆ ◆ ◆

March 15

A relationship can't be healthier than the people in it.

—MARY KAY W.

◆　◆　◆

Some of us left our spouses or partners because of an addiction (drinking, drugging, gambling, spending) and then turned around and found someone else who had the same addiction. We wonder why we didn't learn from our mistakes.

Unless we grow from our misfortune, we will always look for someone to teach us what it is we need to learn. Some of us choose to learn the hard way. Rather than blaming, judging, and criticizing our former spouse or our partner, we examine our own behavior. Why are we drawn to certain types of people? In what ways do we feel inadequate? What gaps are we expecting our partner to fill?

We recognize the gaps and we fill them with self-love. When we do not expect a partner to fill any gaps, we know we're at a place where we feel complete. We find ourselves being drawn to others who also see themselves as whole. We enter a relationship with the ability to give and receive. We still have lessons to learn, but we don't learn them the hard way. We learn in the comfort of a loving relationship.

Today I will see the value in waiting at least a year or two after a divorce or separation before entering into another serious relationship.

◆　◆　◆

March 16

There is no debtor's prison.

—JERROLD MUNDIS

◆　◆　◆

Some of us tend to be melodramatic about our debt. We think and act as if it's the end of the world. Our friends and family will never again respect us. We'll be shamed forever.

We may face lawsuits from creditors, a broken arm from loan sharks, and interest rates that should be a crime, but we will not end up in jail for not paying our debt. We will not face public disgrace. By being in debt we are, in fact, more the norm than the exception.

**Today I will accept that my debt
is not the end of the world.**

◆　◆　◆

March 17

Be aware of wonder.

—Robert Fulghum

◆ ◆ ◆

We have days when we experience the small coincidences in life—our car breaks down and we run into an old friend at the service station; we're thinking about someone and she calls just because we've been on her mind; we ask ourselves a question and the answer appears on the side of a bus or out of the mouth of a stranger at the bus stop. These serendipitous events usually leave us with at least a bit of awe.

The more serendipity we have in our life, the more spiritually connected we are. We're tuned in, attentive, aware, and detached. We're getting responses to questions and meeting the people we need to be with at just the right moments. We couldn't have planned it better. We couldn't have planned it at all. Serendipity is a sign that we're letting the universe organize the events that lead to answered questions and fulfilled dreams. Life becomes a process of unraveling a mystery.

**Today I will recognize the serendipity
in the day's events.**

◆ ◆ ◆

March 18

Where the road bends abruptly, take short steps.

—ERNEST BRAMAH

◆　◆　◆

We sense that we were never meant to have extra money. We decide, for instance, to start using coupons and buying generic products at the grocery store. On our first trip, we saved about fifteen dollars. We're proud of ourselves, until we come home and find an overdraft notice for twenty-five dollars in the mail. We feel we're destined to have only a certain amount of money at any given time. We start thinking that at birth our Higher Power put a dollar amount on our foreheads and that's as much money as we'll ever see in our lifetime.

Abundance is everywhere. No one deserves abundance more than another. It's available to all of us, as much as we want. We check our attitudes and beliefs about money and our fears about never having enough. If we have no fear—if we truly believe that all our needs will be met, every day in every way—we will see and feel abundance. We will remove the blocks we've created, blocks that prevent money from flowing to us.

**Today I will feel freedom in knowing
that abundance is there for the asking.**

◆　◆　◆

March 19

The best way out is always through.

—ROBERT FROST

◆ ◆ ◆

We get bored, lonely, and depressed. We want to change our mood, so we get creative. We think of new things we can bring into our lives, things that will lift our spirits. We go shopping or splurge on a trip or entertainment. Money (or credit) and what it can buy becomes our drug, our mood-altering substance. As with alcohol or cocaine, when the high wears off, our foul mood returns. We haven't addressed the feelings. We've only numbed them temporarily.

The best way to lift our spirits is to work with them, not numb them or drown them out. We allow ourselves to feel our feelings, to get through, rather than around, them. We air our concerns by talking to supportive people. We return to the basics of spirituality—our relationship with self, others, and our Higher Power.

Today I will get to the heart of the matter.

◆ ◆ ◆

March 20

> Whether you think you can or
> whether you think you can't, you're right.
> —HENRY FORD

◆　◆　◆

Usually, if we don't think we can do it, we can't. It's not that we can't—that we're not capable—but that we think we can't. As we think, we believe, and we have a tendency to live by what we believe. We see ourselves as failures. Nobody likes us. We're an embarrassment to the family. So we subconsciously make choices that keep us in that position. If we do start to get ahead careerwise or financially, we sabotage the progress by making more self-defeating choices.

We ask ourselves why we're so down on ourselves. We remember that regardless of how others treat us, we are children of our Higher Power. Our Higher Power believes in us. Our Higher Power put us here to accomplish something. We look for even a kernel of something good in us. We emphasize our strengths, regardless of how big or small. Every day, we remind ourselves of at least one good quality we bring to this planet. We tell ourselves we're worthy of love.

Today I will know I am heaven-sent.

◆　◆　◆

March 21

I didn't make a thousand mistakes in the course of inventing the lightbulb. I simply took a thousand steps.
—THOMAS EDISON

◆ ◆ ◆

Some of us are afraid of change. We're afraid we'll fail, get hurt, do it wrong. To get out of debt, we know we need to do something differently, but we don't know what, exactly. The change we fear might be as little as deciding to balance our checkbook or as big as deciding whether to stay with our partner.

We view change as inventors view inventing—it's a process. It's all trial and error. We try something. If it doesn't work, we've at least learned that it doesn't work. We try another way. It may take us a while to get from point A to point B, but that's okay. Even when we're making mistakes, we're making progress.

Today I will aim for progress, not perfection.

◆ ◆ ◆

March 22

Idealism is fine, but as it approaches reality
the cost becomes prohibitive.
—WILLIAM F. BUCKLEY

◆　◆　◆

After developing an ideal spending plan, we get real by bringing our debt and income into the picture. We take a hard look at our basic needs. These needs may include a vacation every year to a warm climate. Our ideal spending plan may send us to the Bahamas, while our realistic spending plan scales it back to a road trip to a southern state. A realistic spending plan includes a savings account. All planned major and minor purchases will be paid for with cash. Once our basic needs are covered, we see what's left to pay our debts, and if necessary we negotiate lower payments with our creditors.

If we are underearners, a realistic spending plan may motivate us to ask for a raise or to seek job interviews. We know that if our basic needs aren't met, we will return to dysfunctional spending patterns.

Today I will feel empowered knowing that I can have what I need without incurring more unsecured debt.

◆　◆　◆

March 23

There is a serious defect in the thinking of someone who wants—more than anything else—to become rich. As long as they don't have the money, it'll seem like a worthwhile goal. Once they do, they'll understand how important other things are—and have always been.

—JOSEPH BROOKS

◆　◆　◆

Many of us confuse ourselves about where we want to be with money. We may truly abhor the thought of being rich; we associate it with greed and dishonesty. Or we may get disgusted thinking about putting ourselves on some kind of spending plan that limits what we can do, that determines our life for us.

We keep the end goal in mind. The end goal is not to get rich, and it's not to sacrifice. The end goal is to get out of debt so that we—not our debt—can determine how we live our lives.

**Today I will know that being
debt-free is being empowered.**

◆　◆　◆

March 24

Neither God nor the universe has decreed that your
soul has been reduced to second-class status and
your rights stripped away because you owe $3,100.50
to the Pittsburgh First National Bank.

—JERROLD MUNDIS

◆ ◆ ◆

When we're consumed in debt, we live for our
creditors, whether a mortgage company, a host
of credit card companies, or a loan shark. All we think
about is how to pay them. Every spare dime goes to
them. We feel guilty at the thought of spending for our
own pleasure. While we live for creditors or our house,
our lives pass us by. We don't enjoy our days; we stay
awake at night.

We have an obligation and a responsibility to pay our
creditors, but we don't have to act as if they own us.
Every move we make does not have to be based on how
it affects our creditors.

**Today I will accept that responsibility
is not a form of bondage.**

◆ ◆ ◆

March 25

Our belief that others are responsible for our problems and feelings gives away our power to change. When we place the power for our happiness on someone or something that we have no control over, we condemn ourselves to feeling helpless, hurt, and resentful.

—ALLEN A. TIGHE

◆　◆　◆

When we blame others for how we feel, we give them power over us. The truth is that we *decide* to feel hurt, mad, angry, sad, happy, or inadequate. And our decisions are based on what *we* believe.

Empowering ourselves to change how we feel about something or someone requires examining our beliefs. We may believe that we are bad people because of our debting. So when collection agencies badger us at dinnertime, we blame them for the shame and anger we feel. But we need to question the evidence. What is the evidence that being in debt makes us bad people? Surely we're good people in some way—as a parent, spouse, friend, or employee. And what about our expectations? If we think about it, it's reasonable for collection agencies to call during dinnertime, an hour at which most people can be reached.

We, nobody else, determine how we feel. Our decisions are based on our beliefs. We question the logic of our belief system. We take back the power to change how we feel.

Today I will own my feelings.

◆　◆　◆

March 26

The Internet is so big, so powerful and pointless that for some people it is a complete substitute for life.

—ANDREW BROWN

◆　◆　◆

The Internet has opened up a whole new avenue for spenders and gamblers. It's easy and convenient. No one has to know we've been shopping, day-trading, or betting on sports. After all, no one sees us leave the house. We just turn on the computer and log on. It's a surefire way to hide our addiction—until the bills come in.

We view the Internet as a slippery place. We lived without it before, and we can live without it now.

Today I will determine whether my Internet service is a basic need or a slippery place.

◆　◆　◆

March 27

A critic is a creature without a spiritual home, and it is his point of honor never to seek one.

—DESMOND MACCARTHY

◆ ◆ ◆

It's all too easy to decide how others should behave or live their lives. *Should* and *must* are some pretty harsh and rigid words, when we think about it. She *shouldn't* go to the casino. He *must* get a higher-paying job. What we're saying is that we know best, above everyone else and God, about what is right and wrong.

Rather than judge, we choose to observe. We can comment on people's actions and situations—she went to the casino today; he has a low-paying job. But who are we to judge them? If we believe that everything, right now, is as it's supposed to be, we believe that there is a reason people do what they do.

Today I will not judge anyone or anything.

◆ ◆ ◆

March 28

You can tell whether a man is clever by his answers. You can tell whether a man is wise by his questions.

—NAGUIB MAHFOUZ

◆　◆　◆

All we want to do is be debt-free. We don't care if we're wealthy, and we don't care if we can't buy everything we want. All we want at this moment in time is not to have to spend hours paying bills, applying for low-interest credit cards and loans, and figuring out how to get out of this mess. We want to be done with it, and we want to be done with it now.

In our desperation, we may make some hasty decisions that could leave us deeper in debt. We may, for instance, be tempted to withdraw money from an IRA. We say we'll eat the taxes and penalties. We just don't want to have to face the debt. In the end, we end up losing what could have been a sizable tax return as well as a good portion or all of our IRA.

Before we make hasty decisions, we talk to a financial planner or a nonprofit consumer credit counseling service we trust. We discuss our situation and our goals. We listen to reason.

Today I will let patience be my guide.

◆　◆　◆

March 29

Our perception of what's happening and what's really happening are two completely different things.

—UNKNOWN

◆ ◆ ◆

We love how we're treated at the casino. Employees know our name, pit bosses jump when we snap our fingers, and we're always getting vouchers for meals, free tickets for concerts, and complimentary weekends at the hotel. They love us, we're accepted here, we get attention, we belong, we're special. We love how that feels because at home, when we're all alone, we don't feel so special. There's something missing. We feel empty. We go back to the casino to find some action or to fill in the emotional abyss.

Casinos know compulsive gamblers as well as gamblers know their odds. Casinos have us all figured out, and they play on our weaknesses. They give us what we need, or at least act as if they do. Regardless of how we're being treated, we remember we're the same person inside and outside of the casino. We may feel better as we enter the stimulating environment, but as soon as the external stimuli go away, we feel our inner turmoil and emptiness. We can't run from ourselves forever.

Today I will accept that compulsive gambling is a form of escape from my inner self.

◆ ◆ ◆

March 30

Reason is not measured by size
or height but by principle.

—Epictetus

◆　◆　◆

We all have our reasons for wanting to use credit. Credit cards make us feel secure, we may need them for emergencies, they're convenient, and they're in some cases necessary. They're necessary when we have to rent a car, check into a hotel, pay the dentist, or buy a birthday dinner for our mother. Or at least we've convinced ourselves that they are.

Mostly, though, credit cards are necessary when we don't have cash. But we've learned that when we don't have cash (or collateral), we don't spend. The best way to stop using credit cards is not to have any credit cards.

Parting with our beloved credit cards can be hard. We feel like we're taking a risk. We could be out in the world somewhere with nothing, and with no piece of plastic to ensure our safety. The more time we spend without our cards, the more assured we are that all is fine. Believe it or not, we function without them. We cut up our cards. We bury our crutch.

**Today I will stop making excuses
for why I need to carry credit cards.**

◆　◆　◆

March 31

A belief is not merely an idea the mind possesses; it is
an idea that possesses the mind.

—ROBERT OXTON BOLT

◆ ◆ ◆

We *intend* to get out of debt, we *intend* to buy a
house, we *intend* to increase our savings, and we
intend to give to charity. We want to do all of the above,
and we have the best of intentions. So why are we still
in debt, still renting, still without a savings account, and
still afraid to give?

Intentions need the support of our subconscious
mind. We need to believe, deep down and without a
doubt, that we can do and have what we intend. We
may want wholeheartedly to get out of debt, but if we
don't believe it will ever happen, it most likely won't.
We may long for a home of our own, but if we don't
believe we'll be able to handle it, we won't.

**Today I will consider whether my beliefs
are undermining my progress.**

◆ ◆ ◆

April 1

While intelligent people can often simplify the complex,
a fool is more likely to complicate the simple.

—GERALD W. GRUMMET

◆　◆　◆

We tell ourselves we're not interested in learning about money management or investing. It sounds too boring, restrictive, complicated, or time-consuming. Furthermore, we don't care who sells and buys what, we think a blue chip is something we get at a casino or in a gourmet bag of tortillas, and we have no desire to read about the price of pork bellies.

Getting a grip on our personal spending doesn't mean we have to become financial wizards. We don't have to start following the stock market or reading books on economics and investing. All we need to understand is ourselves—our spending patterns and our attitudes toward money—and maybe the concept of compound interest. When we understand our beliefs, we understand our behaviors.

Today I will stop complicating the situation.

◆　◆　◆

April 2

> One of the truths of our time is this hunger
> deep in people all over the planet for coming
> into relationship with each other.
> —MARY CAROLINE RICHARDS

◆　◆　◆

Avoiding people on a regular basis is a sign that we are not dealing with our problems or facing the dark, empty spaces inside. Isolation and withdrawal are symptoms of running away. We think that if we see our family and friends, they'll ask us about our finances. If we're wearing new clothes, they'll judge us for how we're handling our money. We know these are excuses. The truth is we don't want to reveal our secrets, and we know that those who know us best sense when we're covering something up. They'll notice we have empty spaces. They'll see us for what we really are.

Family and friends can be our greatest strengths. With them, we can do what we cannot do alone. With practice, we are able to open up, to unleash our burdens by willingly revealing our mistakes, faults, and humiliations. More often than not, the consequence is greater intimacy.

Today I will not avoid the truth. I will make a meaningful call or visit to one friend or family member.

◆　◆　◆

April 3

Creativity involves breaking out of established patterns
in order to look at things in a different way.

—EDWARD DE BONO

◆　◆　◆

We get wrapped up in our problems to the extent
that they're all we think about. Our attention is
on our problems. We become self-absorbed. What am
I going to do? How am *I* going to get help? Who can
help *me*? Self-centeredness envelops us until we drown
in self-pity, a state of mind that brings us and those
around us down.

We identify our problems and then we focus on finding creative solutions. In doing so, we move forward.

**Today I will affirm that I can
create solutions to my problems.**

◆　◆　◆

April 4

When you're the victim of the behavior, it's black and white; when you're the perpetrator, there are a million shades of gray.

—DR. LAURA SCHLESINGER

◆　◆　◆

The relationships are stereotypical—the righteous boss, the stern parent, and the admonishing police officer. We learn from others that to get something from people we need to be hard on them. We need to show them who's right and who's wrong. We need to put them in their place. We feel we're the victim, and we cry about it by being bossy.

When it comes to our money, we have days—or maybe years—of victimhood, and we take it out on others. Our mind-set is, "I've been without and so you'll be without too!" We believe others should be deprived just as we've been. We see ourselves as victims, but in the end we become perpetrators.

We remember what it means to be on the receiving end of kindness. The better we treat others, the faster we heal, and the better we feel.

**Today I will practice benevolence
in all my thoughts and actions.**

◆　◆　◆

April 5

Life's two Great Questions: Why me?
and What do I do now?

—WILLIAM L. DeANDREA

◆ ◆ ◆

If we're living with an addict who has caused us a great deal of debt (and other grief), we repeatedly ask ourselves, "Why?" Why did this happen to us? We've always been good money managers. We dwell on what we could have done with the lost wages. We think about how both of us are gainfully employed and the house looks like we live in the ghetto. Our cars are falling apart. The neighbors are getting awfully curious about where our spouse spends the nights—why is she always coming home at six o'clock in the morning?

Beware of this kind of thinking and questioning. We need to stop, or we'll drive ourselves crazy and spend endless amounts of energy fighting something we can't battle. The more we resist, the more *it* persists. We're only giving *it* more strength. *It* is addiction, and it can destroy everything beautiful. We look not to what could have been but to what is. We examine our reality. We look for opportunity.

**Today I will stop asking "Why me?"
and start asking "What can I do?"**

◆ ◆ ◆

April 6

You may drive out Nature with a pitchfork,
yet she will hurry back.

—HORACE

◆　◆　◆

One day a loved one comes to us with a problem.
He's got fifty thousand dollars in credit card debt.
If we'd remortgage the house, he'd make the monthly
payment, he'd get a break on interest rates, and we'd
get a tax deduction. Sounds logical enough. We want
to help those we love. We feel we need to be there for
them. We loan them money and co-sign loans. We agree
to sign for low-interest credit cards. We feel anxious and
will do anything to help.

We're in such a whirlwind that all we can think of is
how to get out of today's mess. We need to understand
that the messes will keep coming. We put out one fire,
but there's a much bigger forest still to burn. We look
beyond the immediate and realize that all our efforts
only take us further down the road into debt. We won't
ever be able to put out enough fires because they'll just
keep coming. That's the nature of addiction.

**Today I will know that I am not responsible for
another's debt. I will not interfere with a loved
one's growth and learning by taking care of his
or her debting problems.**

◆　◆　◆

April 7

Faith dares the soul to go farther than it can see.

—WILLIAM CLARK

◆ ◆ ◆

During painful or desperate times, we may feel our Higher Power has abandoned us. We feel empty and hopeless. We give up because all we ever do seems to fail anyway. We feel forsaken. We don't understand why our Higher Power isn't coming to our aid when we so desperately need and want help.

We remember that our Higher Power does not make our decisions for us; it walks with us while we feel our pain so that we may grow and learn compassion. In the darkest of times, we pray, we wait, and we do our best to believe. This simple act is a testament of our faith, even if we don't feel we have any. Out of the darkest hours miracles grow.

Today I will know that I am where I'm supposed to be.

◆ ◆ ◆

April 8

Language exerts hidden power,
like a moon on the tides.

—ALCAEUS

◆　◆　◆

Finances have a way of creeping up in conversations. Regardless of how private we may want to be about our situation, we find ourselves referring to our debt almost daily. "I wish I could afford a trip to the Caribbean"; "I'm so broke"; "We can't buy a house now."

We remember that thoughts and statements are powerful. Thoughts help determine how we feel about ourselves and our situation. Thoughts lead us either to action or inaction. We eliminate *can't* and *never* from our vocabulary. We make truthful, positive statements in the present tense. "I'm paying off my debt"; "My finances are getting in order"; "I'm planning on buying a house." Our thoughts and words begin to work for us.

Today I will be positive and catch and correct any thoughts and words that undermine my progress.

◆　◆　◆

April 9

Some pursue happiness—others create it.

—UNKNOWN

◆ ◆ ◆

Most of us are convinced that a shiny new car, a new dress, or a new computer is going to make us happy. We get so excited thinking about it that we can't imagine not having it in our life. How sad that would be! Before long, the car isn't shiny, the dress doesn't fit, and the computer is obsolete. Our happiness depreciated right along with everything else.

We place the responsibility for our happiness with ourselves, something much more everlasting than a material good. We trust that the best way to be happy is to treat ourselves well, to tell ourselves we're complete as is, and to give happiness to others.

Today I will think of one thing I can do to bring happiness into someone's life.

◆ ◆ ◆

April 10

Learn to become an observer of life
and an observer of self.
—STUART WILDE

❖ ❖ ❖

We're programmed to react to negatives in a certain way. If a collection agent insults us, we're offended. If our child steals from us, we're angry. If our spouse betrays us, we're enraged. We react and put ourselves through emotional highs and lows. Every time someone does something negative to us, we suffer not only because of the deed but also because of the mood it puts us in, which can linger much longer than the consequences of the action.

We can choose to observe rather than react. By becoming an observer, we don't have to feel bad if someone misjudges us, treats us poorly, or accuses us falsely. We simply notice their behavior and leave it at that. It's neither bad nor good; it just is.

Today I will ask myself,
"Who am I hurting when I react?"

❖ ❖ ❖

April 11

You can't be walked on unless you're lying on the floor.
—SYLVIA L.

◆　◆　◆

Defending ourselves diplomatically is a challenge for some of us. We may go overboard, practically pushing others down to get what we feel we deserve. We may try to fool others by using words that don't match our actions. Or, we may want to run and hide from any conflict. When we're in debt—and our self-esteem is down and our anxiety up—it can be hard to find the middle ground. We tend to overreact emotionally, getting upset over small things, or to underreact, feeling hopeless to make a difference.

When we assert ourselves, we raise our self-esteem and lower our anxiety. We know we're making a difference, if only in how we feel about a situation. Being assertive means being honest, direct, and nonjudgmental. We talk calmly, if possible, about how we feel. We use "I feel," not "you did," statements. Being assertive takes practice. We allow ourselves to make mistakes and to come back to the drawing board.

**Today I will avoid using the word
"you" in any argument.**

◆　◆　◆

April 12

Fear less, hope more;
Whine less, breathe more;
Talk less, say more;
Hate less, love more;
And all good things are yours.

—SWEDISH PROVERB

◆ ◆ ◆

After we've taken some time to absorb as much material as we can about getting out of debt and about cutting costs, we determine which methods make the most sense to us given our beliefs and our situation, and we make a plan—not just a financial plan but a life plan.

Making a plan to get out of debt and to create a positive future involves more than deciding how much money to pay to creditors, friends, and relatives every month. It involves reexamining our values, creating worthy goals, and completing our objectives. It involves deciding how much money we'll give to ourselves and to charitable causes. It involves planning for the unexpected. After our financial obligations have been met, it involves investing. More important, it involves living an honorable life. When we do that, good things come to us.

I will plan for the best possible future by acting with honor today.

◆ ◆ ◆

April 13

If you tell the truth, you don't
have to remember anything.
—MARK TWAIN

◆　◆　◆

If we keep our debt a secret—from our spouses, parents, children, close friends—we carry an extremely heavy burden all by ourselves. We feel bad enough for having spent or lost the money in the first place. Our guilt and shame are tripled when we hide all or part of our debt.

We may be afraid of the consequences of revealing our secret. In trying to avoid the consequences (which may or may not happen), we create other, possibly more damaging problems. Those close to us will eventually get to the truth and, knowing they've been lied to, will feel betrayed and enraged. We'll have lost almost all their trust, a fundamental component of healthy relationships.

Rather than be caught like a dog with its tail between its legs, we decide to be honest. We reveal our secrets directly and humbly. In doing so, we unload our burdens.

**Today I will know that by telling others
about my debt, I'm taking a big step
toward solvency and peace of mind.**

◆　◆　◆

April 14

Progress is swapping old troubles for new.
—ANONYMOUS

◆　◆　◆

We continue to look for ways to lower interest rates and, if necessary, to lower monthly payments. If we own a house, we may want to consider consolidating our debt with a low-interest home equity loan. Consolidating can help reduce monthly payments and interest and free up some cash, but we need to remember to treat not only the symptom but also the cause.

A large percentage of people who consolidate find themselves getting deeper and deeper in debt. If we consolidate, we must keep to our spending plan as closely as possible. With a home equity loan, we close all credit card accounts and keep a debit card for purchases where a credit card is required. We remember that consolidation brings us some relief but does not give us permission to maintain poor spending (or earning) patterns.

Today I will remember that consolidation is meant to move me closer to becoming solvent.

◆　◆　◆

April 15

A collision at sea can ruin your entire day.

—THUCYDIDES

◆　◆　◆

We may have five thousand dollars in credit card debt and a high-paying job and just need greater awareness of our spending patterns. We may have a serious gambling, compulsive spending, or drinking and drugging problem that's put us a hundred thousand dollars in the hole. Or, we may be drowning in a sea of medical bills because of a debilitating chronic illness. To others, our troubles may appear big or small, but when we're in the midst of them, we tend to view them as catastrophic.

Regardless of the size of our debt, we feel consequences. We give up serenity, happiness, and hope. We feel inadequate and possibly enraged. In the scheme of things, however, debt itself is a small matter. We work on our perspective and decide whether we'll let our debt ruin a day or a lifetime.

Today I will emotionally detach myself from my debt; I will not treat my debt as if it's as important as life itself.

◆　◆　◆

April 16

Money is just what we use to keep tally.

—HENRY FORD

◆　◆　◆

The square footage of our house, the make and model of our car, the size of our TV screens, the power of our computers, and the designers of our clothes—all these things and more show the outside world how much money we have (however deceiving that may be!). They to some extent also indicate the value we put on possessions. Some of us may just take for granted that having the biggest, the best, or the most is what we should want and expect.

If we change our thinking, we eliminate some agony. More doesn't necessarily mean better. Excess stuff drains our energy. Living in an environment that reflects not how much money we have but who we are satisfies our souls. It's uplifting. In redirecting our focus, we lose our desire to spend money.

Today I will reevaluate my environment. I will donate or sell at least as many items as equals my age. I will strive to have less rather than more.

◆　◆　◆

April 17

[Self-control is] coolness and absence of heat and haste.
—RALPH WALDO EMERSON

◆ ◆ ◆

When we're out of milk or bread, we may stop at the convenience store on the way home from work. Not only do we pay more money than we'd pay in a grocery store, but we also pick up bubble gum for the kids, some lottery tickets, and a cup of coffee or a soda pop. We've only planned on spending a few dollars but leave with ten or fifteen dollars worth of goods—more than twice what we'd intended.

We pick one day of the week to grocery shop. We have something in our stomachs before we go. If possible, we go without the kids. We keep a list and stick to it as much as possible. We don't return until the same day next week. If we run out of tissue or bread or milk, we get creative and try to do without and plan better for our next shopping trip.

Today I will decide which day of the week is for grocery shopping and determine where to keep my ongoing grocery list.

◆ ◆ ◆

April 18

Any activity becomes creative when the doer
cares about doing it right, or doing it better.

—JOHN UPDIKE

◆ ◆ ◆

Most of us spend a fair amount of money on food. Most of us also discard a fair amount of spoiled fruit, vegetables, and leftovers every week. If that's the case, our grocery bill is one of the first places we can look to cut costs.

We become intimately familiar with what's in our refrigerator and freezer, and we plan to use it. Some of us plan meals a week in advance, or we at least know in the morning what we're going to eat for each meal of that day. As we get better at planning meals, we get better at shopping for the right type and amount of foods.

**Today I will be creative—not wasteful—
with the perishable foods in my house.**

◆ ◆ ◆

April 19

Wealth can't buy health, but health can buy wealth.
—HENRY DAVID THOREAU

◆ ◆ ◆

Busy parents are often, if not most of the time, rushing to throw together lunches. We buy prepackaged soups, pastas, juices, or whatever else we can think of to give some variety and to save time.

We may be saving time, but possibly only a few minutes a day. Instead of regularly spending money on prepackaged foods loaded with sodium and other preservatives, we make healthy, cost-cutting choices. We can spend some time on the weekend preparing fresh soup or pasta, immediately freezing it in serving-size containers for the week, and can pack it for lunches. We use thermoses or refillable plastic containers for juice or milk. We get healthy meals, and we save money.

Today I will make conscious, healthy, cost-cutting choices when planning lunches for school or work.

◆ ◆ ◆

April 20

Penny wise, pound foolish.

—ROBERT BURTON

◆　◆　◆

We can become so cost-conscious that we end up doing just the opposite, spending more rather than less. We want to install a new kitchen floor. Instead of saving up a little longer to buy a durable floor, we buy the cheapest vinyl on the market, thinking we're saving hundreds of dollars. We don't want to take the time to save more money. After two years, our floor is worn in high-traffic areas and dented by chair legs. Sooner or later, we end up dishing out even more money.

We don't always need to have the best, but we learn to know when paying more up front is a wise investment. Before purchasing, we learn about the warranties and guarantees. We think it through. We accept that spending a lot of money on high-quality products can be a wise, cost-saving expenditure over time.

Today I will recognize when I'm being pound foolish.

◆　◆　◆

Let us live simply so that others may simply live.
—MOTHER ELIZABETH ANN SETON

◆　◆　◆

In the United States, we are 5 percent of the world's population, yet we consume 82 percent of the world's raw materials. When we cut back on consumption and simplify cleaning products (for example, by using vinegar instead of chemically based products), we are not only saving money, we're also helping to save the environment. Every time we decide not to buy a material good or a prepackaged food, we can think about *all* we're saving and feel doubly good. We don't feel deprived; we're making a contribution.

Today I will feel gratified knowing I make conscious choices about my immediate environment and about the environment at large.

◆　◆　◆

April 22

Buckminster Fuller calculated that if all the wealth of the world were divided equally among its citizens, each and every one of us would be a millionaire. . . .

The things that get in our way are feelings of lack, despair, and confusion; and the inability to master the marketplace of life.

—STUART WILDE

❖ ❖ ❖

We drive by hearty crops on a rolling countryside, past tall pines, lush fruit trees, colorful flowers, or sparkling waters. When we're with nature, we see and feel the abundance. When we drive through poverty-stricken neighborhoods with dilapidated homes and buildings, we see and feel lack and need.

When we start out with the notion that the world already offers us everything we'll ever need and more, we start out with the notion that abundance is there for us and ultimately within reach. We take the first step of believing that abundance is ours if we truly want it.

Today I will spend some time alone in nature to feel the abundance.

❖ ❖ ❖

April 23

What lies behind us and what lies before us are tiny matters compared to what lies within us.

—RALPH WALDO EMERSON

◆　◆　◆

Not being able to take advantage of opportunities to travel or to buy expensive items can make us feel "less than." We compare ourselves with others. "If so-and-so can make it, why can't I?" Our debt and all the issues we surround it with loom over us. We feel that others look at us as though we're different.

Instead of creating a sea of fear and doubt, we tell ourselves we're worthy. This is simply a growth season. We make the most of it by learning to believe in ourselves. No matter what life brings us, we can call on the strength and courage within us to rise above it. We accept ourselves as we are now. We are born adequate. If we look within, we will find the strength, courage, and wisdom we need to make the right choices at the right time.

Today I will tell myself I am capable over and over again.

◆　◆　◆

April 24

When you help someone today,
someone will help you tomorrow.

—MAMA D.

◆　◆　◆

We need a new roof. The carpet needs shampoo-ing. The pipes are leaking. The house needs painting. Big and small projects around the house, whether costly or not, can drain a pocketbook fast. Being able to call on friends, neighbors, a support group, and family for help can save loads of time, energy, and money. But how do we not feel guilty ask-ing for free labor? How do we get to a point where these acts help to bond us rather than create resentments and separate us?

Each of us is talented in one way or another. We may be a whiz at installing carpet, sewing, investing, writ-ing, or painting. We may own some special equip-ment—a carpet shampooer, a sander, or a spray painter. When we need to get a project done, we ask not only who can help us but also what can we do in exchange.

**Today I will think about what talents or
equipment I have that I can share with others.**

◆　◆　◆

April 25

Animals are creatures that lead silence through the world of man and language and are always putting silence down in front of man. . . . Animals move through the world like a caravan of silence. . . . The silence of animals and the silence of nature would not be so great and noble if it were merely a failure of language to materialize.

—MAX PICARD

◆　◆　◆

Many of us live and work in a city, or we return to a bedroom community after a long day at the office. Most of our time is spent sitting in a windowless, ventilated office and on the road. When we get to our driveways, some of us press the button to the garage door opener, park the car, and enter the house. We spend only minutes outdoors. We don't talk to our neighbors.

We've adapted to these artificial settings, but we cannot separate ourselves from nature forever. We are a part of nature, and nature is a part of us. By separating ourselves from nature, we feel less than whole. To commune with nature, to meditate and to observe, is to become whole again. To spend time by ourselves, in nature and in silence, is an extremely powerful healing experience. In silence and in nature, we know that it is no accident that animals don't talk.

Today I will spend time alone in nature.

◆　◆　◆

April 26

It is an old and ironic habit of human beings
to run faster when we have lost our way.

—ROLLO MAY

♦   ♦   ♦

Debt is chaos. We don't know exactly how much
money we have because we haven't filed our
papers or balanced our checkbook. We don't know how
much debt we have or how long it will take us to pay
it off because we can't seem to let our minds settle
enough to get beyond worrying about how to pay the
next bill. We're in a tizzy, going nowhere fast.

We slow down and get centered. We can do this several ways. We take deep breaths, stretch, soak up some
sun, take a long walk or a hot bath, or connect with
nature. Slowing down can be simple.

Today I will find one way to slow down.

♦   ♦   ♦

April 27

Like other compulsions, compulsive debting feeds
on itself: the more you do it, the more problems
that inevitably result; the more problems that result,
the more you do it to obtain relief from these new
problems.

—JERROLD MUNDIS

◆　◆　◆

Once we're in debt, we enact behaviors that help us avoid the problem until it grows to unmanageable levels. Many of us can identify with at least a few debting behaviors. Are we ever behind on payments? Do we hide bills in a drawer? Is our checking account unbalanced? Do we wait until the last minute to mail payments? Do we make minimum payments? Do we feel mature and successful when we use a credit card? Are we only vaguely familiar with the terms of our credit cards—that is, do we know only the interest rate and credit limit? Do we keep our debt a secret?

Any and all of the above behaviors feed the cycle of debt. To break it, we accept that our debting has made our lives unmanageable. We turn the problem over to our Higher Power and ask for guidance.

Today I will accept that unless I make some changes, my debting problem will only get worse.

◆　◆　◆

April 28

Behavior is a mirror, in which
everybody shows his image.
—JOHANN W. GOETHE

◆ ◆ ◆

Debt is a noun. The dictionary does not list the word debt as a verb—"to debt," "debting." According to the dictionary, debt is a condition, a state of being, not an action.

But spending money is an action. And spending money we don't have is an action we need to be able to readily identify. In our heads, at least, we can use the word *debting* to refer to our behavior when we're incurring unsecured debt. We're not spending, we're not shopping, we're not avoiding our bills, we're not gambling, we're not taking another day off without pay because of a hangover—we're debting.

**Today I will start using the word "debting"
to describe behaviors and spending patterns
that incur more unsecured debt.**

◆ ◆ ◆

April 29

Freedom is like taking a bath—
you have to keep doing it every day!
—FLO KENNEDY

◆　◆　◆

We reach a point in our lives when we decide to change, or when some event or circumstance propels us into change. This choice marks a period of growth. It is preceded by agony—the pain is so intense we cannot possibly stay where we are. Our souls cry for a better way of being. We have no choice but to change. When the dust settles, however, our memories fade. We occasionally slip into our old behaviors. We don't have time to meditate, and we convince ourselves we don't need to record *every* expense.

To recover from a slip, we admit we're slipping, and we look back to when we first determined we had a problem. What books did we read? What friends did we consult? Did we need to attend support group meetings? What about therapy? How's our relationship with our Higher Power? We get back on track. We stay free by returning daily to our tried and true sources of inspiration.

**Today I will sustain the spiritual growth
and freedom I've achieved by remembering
what I did to achieve it.**

◆　◆　◆

April 30

The universe operates through dynamic exchange . . .
giving and receiving are different aspects of the flow
of energy in the universe. And in our willingness to give
that which we seek, we keep the abundance of the
universe circulating in our lives.

—DEEPAK CHOPRA

◆　◆　◆

The word *currency* comes from the Latin word *currere,* which means "to run," as in "to flow." Currency, of course, is another term for money. By definition, money is meant to be exchanged. We give and receive it. We've probably all heard the expressions "What goes around comes around"; "Give and you shall receive"; "You get what you give." We've probably all experienced this phenomenon as well, sometimes with surprise or even amazement.

When we feel we're lacking, we open our hearts to giving. When we give what we seek, we find it returns to us at the right time and place—just when we need it, reminding us that we do not lack for anything. Gifts needn't be material or verbal. They can be good thoughts and prayers, affection, or time.

**Today I will give joyfully,
knowing that my needs will be met.**

◆　◆　◆

May 1

Your vision will become clear only when you look
into your heart. Who looks outside . . . dreams.
Who looks inside, awakens.

—CARL JUNG

◆　◆　◆

Just as we may look to an outside source to blame
for our debt, we may also look to an outside source
to get us out of debt. We wait for someone or something to come in and make everything better. We're in
a perpetual state of anticipation. "If only my ex would
see the kids regularly, I could take a second job and
stop paying for sitters." "If my mom would agree to
remortgage her house, I could consolidate." "When I
hit the jackpot, I'll pay off my debt and everyone
else's."

Asking for emotional support is an excellent, healthy
way to get through difficult times. We cross the line
when we expect others to meet our challenges for us.
Regardless of how unjust the situation may seem to us,
we stop waiting for a knight in shining armor or a streak
of good luck. We have faith in ourselves and our Higher
Power—a force that gives us the strength to take our
own action. We are independent and empowered to
make changes. We find strength in knowing our circumstances and in working from there. In this way, we
may even find the courage to alter an unjust situation.

**Today I will feel the freedom in knowing that I'm
empowered to make a positive difference in my life.**

◆　◆　◆

May 2

Sometimes the question is not
"What do we want?" but "What can we give?"
—ANONYMOUS

◆ ◆ ◆

Some of us wake up every day wondering who's going to help us. How are we going to get out of this mess? We get depressed. Instead of enjoying the moment, we worry about the future or curse the past. We become consumed by our troubles. Our expectations of others are either unrealistic or unknown to them. We live in silent desperation. When our expectations go unfulfilled, we are discontent.

The best way to get help is to give help. We shift from self-pity to self-fulfillment. We reach out to others in need. We see and feel ourselves as not needing. We have something to give. In this simple act alone, we experience joy.

Today I will ask, How can I help?

◆ ◆ ◆

May 3

During challenging circumstances,
I will move forward, not backward.
—STUART WILDE

◆　◆　◆

We have a lot to complain about—the pressures of mounting bills, deteriorating health, spouses, former spouses, kids, relatives, the car, and the plumbing. Worry, worry, worry. We let our troubles interfere with our serenity. We're crabby with the kids, our spouse, or the dog. We question why nothing seems to go our way. We believe we've been doing all the right things, yet we're not being rewarded with happiness. What happened to the good times, we ask? Don't we deserve some? When we wallow in self-pity, we get depressed, and we move backward.

We accept that suffering is part of our personal evolution. We can feel the pain and still find the strength to move forward—to evolve. We consider what we can do about the stack of bills and the clunky car. We realize maybe it's time to discipline ourselves, to start taking the bus! When we think in terms of moving forward, optimism automatically sets in. Forward action becomes intrinsic.

Today I will move forward.

◆　◆　◆

May 4

Strong lives are motivated by dynamic purposes.
—KENNETH HILDEBRAND

◆ ◆ ◆

Some days we wonder where we're going and what we're doing here. Nothing feels right. We're restless and discontented.

When life feels like it's going nowhere, we examine our values, priorities, and goals, which all add up to give us a purpose in life. If we've thought them through carefully and listened to our inner voice, we can be confident we're headed in the right direction. With purpose we have strength.

Because we are creative, sometimes our purpose is several layers thick. A value, for instance, may be community, a priority may be to live in a close-knit community, and a goal may be to organize a community event. If we combine this goal with our goal to pay off our debt, we may decide to organize a citywide garage sale. We get community and money at the same time.

Today I will know that having purpose in my life is only a few thoughts away.

◆ ◆ ◆

May 5

The great thing in this world is not so much
where we are but in what direction we are moving.
—OLIVER WENDELL HOLMES JR.

◆ ◆ ◆

Even with all our systems in place, we get discouraged, even depressed. No amount of purpose or goals seems to be enough. We become mentally, emotionally, and spiritually paralyzed, unable or unwilling to move forward. Our goals feel heavy, uninspired, or out of reach; the work too hard or overwhelming. Do we really want what we're after? Will we even feel any joy when we reach our goal?

We stay in the present moment, being mindful of the tasks at hand, and giving them our heart and soul. All the while, we keep the overall purpose in mind. We don't obsess; we just remember what we're working toward. We believe in it, and it gives us strength. Our mentality is one of a brave warrior; we perform with honor and utter confidence in our mission. We keep our heads up, out of today's muck, and toward the future.

Today I will know that my purpose is divine.

◆ ◆ ◆

May 6

It is good to have an end to journey toward,
but it is the journey that matters, in the end.

—URSULA K. LE GUIN

◆ ◆ ◆

Why is it that when we achieve some goals, we don't feel much excitement or joy? Having a goal can sustain us with strength and purpose for long periods of time. When we finally reach our goal, we sit back and wonder what to do next. How will we occupy our time? Reaching the goal may have been hard work, yet that is what kept us going. It was the process, not the product that mattered. So, in the end, we may even feel a bit down.

We remember that we have more goals on our agenda and mentally prepare to start tackling them. But before we plunge ahead, we pause to reap the rewards of achieving our milestone. We take time to acknowledge our achievement, to remember our sacrifices and hard work, to remember the joy of the process, to thank those who've helped us along the way. We celebrate.

**Today I will remember that rewards
can sustain us as much as having goals.**

◆ ◆ ◆

May 7

An optimist expects his dreams to come true;
a pessimist expects his nightmares to.

—LAWRENCE J. PETER

◆ ◆ ◆

We wake up tired and grumpy, drag ourselves to the shower, get the kids ready for school, and walk into work with a frown. Today is just another day of routine and debt. Nothing will change. We're bound to live each and every day this way. That's just the way it is. We might as well accept it. Nothing's going to get better.

Pessimism *is* a nightmare. Optimism works wonders. Believing we have a chance and that things will work out for the best gives us the stamina we need to get the results we want, or at least the best results possible. When we're optimistic, we attract a positive energy— hope. People want to be around us. People want the best for us.

Today I will be optimistic.

◆ ◆ ◆

May 8

Veracity does not consist in saying,
but in the intention of communicating truth.

—SAMUEL TAYLOR COLERIDGE

◆　◆　◆

People are motivated by many factors: money, love, desire, fame, passion, ignorance, peace—the list goes on. When we're motivated we usually take positive action. Sometimes we get what we want and feel good about it. Other times, we get what we want but feel miserable.

When something feels so right we think it can't be wrong (yet we end up in worse shape emotionally), we need to question our intention. If it is to get rich or get even or is not well thought out, we're most likely creating more negativity in our lives. If we intend only goodness, our intentions are pure and the outcome is always happiness.

**Today I will place pure goodness
behind every action.**

◆　◆　◆

May 9

One's life story cannot be told with complete veracity.
A true autobiography would have to be written in
states of mind, emotions, heartbeats, smiles, and tears;
not in months and years, or physical events. Life is
marked off on the soul by feelings, not by dates.

—HELEN ADAMS KELLER

◆　◆　◆

Most of us define ourselves by what we do or even
by what condition we might have. We're stock-
brokers, marketers, housewives, salespeople, or waiters;
we're retired or chronically ill; we're alcoholics or drug
addicts, gamblers, codependents, compulsive spenders,
or underearners.

Are we what we do or are we what we feel? The less
we feel about ourselves, the more we act compulsively.
We've denied ourselves our feelings, so we treat ourselves to the blackjack table, the bigger house, and the
faster car.

Sometimes we need to process anger or hurt before
sharing. But being able to openly express how we feel
about someone or something indicates that we're in
touch with our feelings and that we feel good enough
about ourselves to say something when we're hurt—or
when we're happy.

**Today I will embrace, respect,
and honor my feelings.**

◆　◆　◆

May 10

I salute the God who dwells within you.

—NEPALESE EXPRESSION

◆   ◆   ◆

In Nepal, one word—*namasté*—expresses an entire sentence in English. The word is used to acknowledge and give gratitude for the God-given light within each of us. To hear *namasté,* one does not need to be a great hero, be well known, have a high IQ, or be wealthy or prominent. *Namasté* is for all of us.

We know we are worthy of giving and receiving such an honorable acknowledgment. We honor the strength, courage, and wisdom of the God within us.

Today I will know that I am defined neither by the size of my bank account nor by the size of my debt, but by the strength of my spirituality.

◆   ◆   ◆

May 11

Everybody thinks of changing humanity
and nobody thinks of changing himself.

—LEO TOLSTOY

◆　◆　◆

Times change. It no longer takes one month to cross the Atlantic, we don't have to brew our own root beer, and we don't need to visit a tailor to have an outfit sewn. Technology and credit equal instant gratification. Some of us reminisce about how much better it was in simpler times. Others argue that we have far more leisure time now that we have everything at our fingertips.

Our evolution as a people is neither good nor bad; it simply is. We are where we are as a whole for a reason. Rather than criticize the way things are done today, we look at the person in the mirror. When we change for the better, even in microscopic ways, the results spread and magnify.

**Today I will focus on one thing I can do
to improve my relationships with others.**

◆　◆　◆

May 12

Aim for fairness!
—DOROTHY L.

◆　◆　◆

Do we have family financial goals? Are we planning to buy a house or a car, or to take a family vacation? Who makes these decisions? Does one person dominate what happens to the money? Are family members in the dark or informed?

We evaluate our family environment regarding finances. When we create an environment where it's safe to talk about money, when we feel knowledgeable, when we know there are no secrets, when we feel we have a say, when our children are learning about responsible choices, we create a feeling in the family of possibilities and of richness.

Today I will consider the benefits of involving my family in financial decisions.

◆　◆　◆

May 13

> The simple act of conversing with your child
> can work wonders. . . . Conversation provides one
> of the best routes to a good relationship.

—LOUIS BATES AMES AND FRANCES L. ILG

◆　◆　◆

We teach our kids about the danger of drugs and alcohol, to stay away from strangers, and not to play with fire. All of this is done with their best interests in mind. It's important to their survival, to their ability to make the right choices for themselves, and to their ability to thrive as human beings. But what do we teach them about money?

Our children learn a lot from what we do. They may in fact be emulating our spending patterns. While we can't be perfect, we can take steps to make sure our kids have the money management skills they'll need to survive. If we don't know where to begin, we consider enrolling them in classes offered free by the Consumer Credit Counseling Service (CCCS) or other nonprofit organizations.

Today I will think of one way to communicate with children about healthy money management.

◆　◆　◆

May 14

The reason people blame things on the previous generations is that there's only one other choice.

—DOUG LARSON

◆　◆　◆

As parents, we are responsible for providing for our children. Even if we give them an allowance in exchange for doing chores, most of us know we're going to end up shelling out money on clothes, music, toys, and entertainment. We're going to "give" them the money in one way or another. To an extent, it's our responsibility. Why not take the opportunity to also give them the skills they'll need to manage money for themselves?

An allowance encourages our children to manage money. We determine how much money we will *give* them without asking for anything in exchange. We give young children a piggy bank; we take school-age children to the bank, where they can deposit a certain amount of their allowance into a savings account; we give teenagers a clothing budget and let them determine whether they want brand names or quantity. We let the kids make wish lists of what they want to save for. We allow kids to trust themselves and to be responsible for their own behavior.

Today I will allow my children to be responsible for their own money.

◆　◆　◆

May 15

Responsibility simply means, the ability to respond.
—JOHN-ROGER AND PETER McWILLIAMS

◆ ◆ ◆

We may dread trips to the department store because we know we're going to hear the inevitable "Can I have a toy?" Our kids know we don't want to yell or bicker in public. They know, and they use their knowledge to get what they want.

Instead of saying no or arguing with our children, we kindly agree. Yes, agree—but not to buying the toy. We agree that the doll is beautiful or the action figure is cool, and then we put their spending plans in action. We suggest that they put the items on their wish list of things to buy with their allowance. If the item is expensive and if we're willing, we could offer to pay for half once they've saved up the money. We put the ball in our children's court. They decide.

Today I will allow my children to be responsible for some of their own decisions.

◆ ◆ ◆

May 16

Fear is the start of wisdom.

—MIGUEL DE UNAMUNO

◆　◆　◆

When we give up our credit cards, we need to carry cash, but a lot of us are afraid to. We fear we may get robbed, lose our wallet, or discover a hole in our pocket.

Getting robbed and forgetting our wallet do not happen to us every day. To get past our fear—or the unfamiliarity of carrying cash—we experiment. We carry different amounts of cash on different days. We discover the dollar amount we're most comfortable carrying.

**Today I will pay attention to my feelings
when putting cash in my wallet.**

◆　◆　◆

May 17

> The art of being wise is the art
> of knowing what to overlook.
> —WILLIAM JAMES

◆ ◆ ◆

We feel the slightest discomfort in our lives and think of a material solution. Wouldn't it be nice to furnish the entire house at once? Why live without? We decide we have to buy it, and we have to buy it now. Reflex spending is spending without thinking through *all* the consequences. We notice the positive consequences—how much fun we'll have, how nice the house will look. Buying on credit is almost always reflex spending. We go for instant gratification rather than thinking of the long-term impact on our finances.

We choose instead to find pleasure in the process of earning and saving for what we want. When we buy reflexively, we clutter our space with goods we find we really didn't care for after all. By waiting, we discover what it is we truly need and want.

Today I will wait at least twenty-four hours before deciding whether to make an unexpected (impulse) purchase.

◆ ◆ ◆

May 18

Vanity is the quicksand of reason.

—GEORGE SAND

◆　◆　◆

At certain points during the aging process we notice changes in our bodies that can actually frighten us. All of a sudden, it seems, we have more wrinkles, droops, gray hairs, stretch marks, cellulite, and bulges. We panic, maybe more so if we're divorced and dating or in a career that requires us to look youthful. We tell ourselves we'll do whatever it takes. We make frequent trips to the plastic surgeon and buy expensive anti-aging creams.

Beauty may be one of our priorities. While attending to beauty needs is fine, we need to consider our financial picture. We think it through before making a purchase or an appointment.

Today I will think of ways to spend less on beauty and concentrate on finding the beauty within.

◆　◆　◆

May 19

I cling to my imperfection,
as the very essence of my being.

—ANATOLE FRANCE

◆　◆　◆

If we react to advertising messages about beauty, comparing ourselves with others who are either younger or naturally more "youthful," we can get depressed and desperate.

We look at our self-esteem, the real cause of our discontent. We tell ourselves the truth. We were made this way. We are lovable just the way we are. Others can sense when we accept ourselves; when others know we're okay with the way we are, they respond in kind.

Our feelings about our appearance may be our ticket to finding greater self-esteem, to recognizing the beauty within. If others truly disdain or judge us for our physical appearance, we know that they need to look at their own self-esteem.

**Today I will know that humble self-assurance
without perfection radiates more beauty and
uniqueness than pretension.**

◆　◆　◆

May 20

If you dam a river it stagnates.
Running water is beautiful water. So be a channel.

—ENGLISH PROVERB

◆　◆　◆

Our thoughts basically take place on three levels. On the lowest, least productive level are negative, or *wasteful,* thoughts. On the next level are the practical thoughts—today we need to balance the checkbook, stop at the grocery store, and call a client. On the highest level are positive thoughts, which direct our attention and intention toward positive outcomes.

When we think about our debt, we think in positive terms: What behavior can I change? How can I increase my income? How can I simplify? Positive thoughts move us forward. When we dwell on the negative, we stay in the negative.

Today, whenever I think a negative thought, I will tell myself to move on to the next thought.

◆　◆　◆

May 21

When people envy me I think, Oh God,
don't envy me; I have my own pains.
—BARBRA STREISAND

♦ ♦ ♦

We see people who seem happy, who seem to have their life together, who have success and talent, and we wish we were them. Or we wish we had what they had. The grass looks greener on the other side.

When we're envious, we're usually looking to fill a gap. We remember that appearances are deceiving. People feel whole at times but not always. None of us is perfect; none of us is meant to be perfect. We're here to make progress.

Today, when I envy someone, I will realize there's more than meets the eye.

♦ ♦ ♦

May 22

Where observation is concerned,
chance favors only the prepared mind.

—LOUIS PASTEUR

◆ ◆ ◆

Many of us find it easier to keep track of our money if we open a separate checking account for variable, unexpected, and occasional expenses. We look at our spending plan to see how much we've determined we can reasonably spend on vacations, clothing, and entertainment—the variable expenses. We calculate how much we'll need for the occasional expenses—car insurance, taxes, gifts, house paint, and trips to the doctor, dentist, or veterinarian. Finally, we anticipate car maintenance and repair or the need to buy a new washing machine.

We add up the dollar amount, divide it by twelve, and know how much to deposit each month in our separate account. We keep detailed records of our spending in every category and the balance remaining in our account for each particular category.

Today I will look to money management sources for tips on record-keeping or will devise my own expense tracking sheets.

◆ ◆ ◆

May 23

Defeat is not the worst of failures.
Not to have tried is the true failure.

—GEORGE E. WOODBERRY

◆　◆　◆

On top of daily living expenses and variable, occasional, and unexpected expenses, we may encounter *major* unexpected expenses. We get laid off, we need surgery, we need to take time off work to take care of our parents, the basement floods, a tree falls on top of the deck, we have a bad case of termites in the house. The list goes on and on.

We may tell ourselves we don't want to think that far ahead. Why worry about something that hasn't happened? We're having enough trouble dealing with today's bills; why should we imagine new troubles?

Unless we're prepared for them, unexpected expenses are the surest way to get us debting again. We can't predict what will happen or when, but we can do our best to be financially prepared for emergencies. We have a savings account specifically for contingencies—life's major unexpected expenses. The amount we put into this account is a personal decision, but many financial advisers recommend saving three to six months' worth of income. If a catastrophe never takes place, we're that much ahead.

**Today I will accept that planning for
the unexpected does not make me paranoid;
it keeps me ahead of the game.**

◆　◆　◆

May 24

Fears and doubts get smaller when we talk about them.

—ANONYMOUS

◆ ◆ ◆

We've been religious about recording our daily expenses. We've heightened our money awareness to a point where we're able to make sound decisions regarding our finances. We're creative about how to cut costs and about finding ways to make more money. We haven't gambled or missed a day's work in six months. We think we're doing pretty good.

We still, however, have nagging urges and desires to go back to our old behaviors. After all, gambling or shopping was our way of life for years. We don't just change overnight.

When we're feeling low or tempted to overspend, we call a support person. We tell him or her exactly what it is we want to do. The simple act of expressing thoughts can actually diminish their power. Instead of repeating them over and over in our heads, we share them. It's the difference between hiding something we're ashamed of and humbly revealing our weaknesses.

Today, when I'm tempted to return to old behaviors, I will call someone.

◆ ◆ ◆

May 25

Nor is the people's judgment always true:
The most err as grossly as the few.
—JOHN DRYDEN

◆　◆　◆

Some of us who are financially and spiritually bankrupt because of another's addiction to gambling, alcohol, or drugs may take on a sort of "holier than thou" attitude. Our lives have been so devastated that we see gambling or drinking as evil. We begin to judge others for participating in such behaviors.

We remember that some people can drink or gamble socially. They have one or two drinks, lose a predetermined amount of money at the slot machines, and leave. They had a good time. They got a break. They were entertained. Although addiction wreaks havoc on a countless number of lives, the world is full of "nonaddicts."

Today I will not let knowing what I know about addiction cause me to judge others.

◆　◆　◆

May 26

The most disturbing and wasteful emotions
in modern life, next to fright, are those which
are associated with the idea of blame, directed
against the self or against others.

—MARILYN FERGUSON

◆ ◆ ◆

Some of us are so outraged by the effect gambling has
had on society that we take on the attitude of a pro-
hibitionist, believing that casinos and lotteries should
be outlawed.

While reducing access to casinos and lotteries can be
a worthwhile cause, it does little to help people who are
already consumed in their addiction. Instead of blaming the conduit, we focus on renewing the spirit of the
addict. We acknowledge that the addict needs emotional and spiritual help. If all we do is take away casinos, the compulsive gambler will turn to illegal
gambling or to another external "cure," maybe drugs
or suicide.

**Today I will acknowledge that
each of us makes our own choices.**

◆ ◆ ◆

May 27

We must dare to think "unthinkable" thoughts.
We must learn to explore all the options and possibilities
that confront us in a rapidly changing world.

—WILLIAM FULBRIGHT

◆ ◆ ◆

If we live with someone who's addicted to gambling, spending, alcohol, or drugs, we may not know what to do. We may be deep in debt as a result of the addiction, but our feelings for our spouse are still strong. We don't want to break up the marriage. We want to work it out. But in saving our marriage, how can we save our finances?

If our spouse is still debting because of an addiction, this could put us in dire straits financially, but breaking up the marriage is not the only out. We need to find out what our legal options are. Some couples divorce only on paper but continue to live as a married couple. This is one way to protect ourselves from abominable financial hardship—an option we may or may not be open to.

Members of Gam-Anon and Al-Anon, support groups for people affected by the behaviors of gamblers and alcoholics, can help us by sharing how they manage to stay with an addicted partner.

**Today I will consider where I'm
willing to draw the line financially.**

◆ ◆ ◆

May 28

For some reason, any reason in the world, life owes you.
—JERROLD MUNDIS

◆　◆　◆

We had a great day at work; we had a bad day at work. We passed the exam; we failed the exam. We won the game; we lost the game. We had a pleasant day with the kids; we had a rough day with the kids. Our spouse left for the weekend; our spouse came home for the weekend. We find a reason, any reason, to spend. We feel entitled to a purchase. Life owes us something, by golly, and we're going to go get it.

We acknowledge that we deserve rewards and celebrations. By definition, however, rewards and celebrations are special occurrences. The big ones don't happen every day. While it can be wonderful to recognize the smaller hurdles and accomplishments in life, we make a choice to reward and celebrate them in proportion to their significance. A pat on the back or a prayer of gratitude to our Higher Power will do in a pinch.

Today I will feel entitled to the rewards earned through responsible behavior.

◆　◆　◆

May 29

Quality will get you through times of no money better than money will get you through times of no quality.

—UNKNOWN

◆　◆　◆

Once we're out of the muck, progressing with our payments, feeling good about our behavior, we start living high-quality days. We may be dirt poor, but it doesn't matter. We have faith in ourselves and our future. We feel good about our choices.

If and when we reach a point where we're gaining monetary wealth, we check our behavior and spirituality. We acknowledge that money alone does not bring good times and that we need to place relationships above all else. Good times are made up of quality relationships and of feeling good about ourselves and our behavior.

Today I will look at quality, not quantity.

◆　◆　◆

May 30

Do not veil the truth with falsehood,
nor conceal the truth knowingly.

—THE KORAN

❖ ❖ ❖

Our mind-set is, "Someday, everything will be fine." We work extra jobs, cut whatever expenses we can, and live in a perpetual state of oblivion. We don't look at reality; it's too painful. We don't want to see our or our loved one's addiction, whether it's gambling, drinking, drugging, or compulsive spending, as being a permanent condition. We think he or she will change—someday. So, we wait and hope, but someday never comes.

When we see people and situations for what they truly are, our someday rolls around. It may not be the rosy picture we'd imagined, but we escape our bondage to the belief that everything will be fine if we just wait. We need to do more than wait. We need to see the addict's behavior for what it truly is—an addiction he or she has no control over. When we accept that the addict won't change if we keep enabling, we change. When we change, *someday* starts to happen.

Today I will see my freedom in the truth.

❖ ❖ ❖

May 31

Nothing happens unless first a dream.

—CARL SANDBURG

✦ ✦ ✦

What do we see when we daydream about the future? Is everything much better than it is now, or are we still struggling with the same money issues? Are we dreaming about what we really want or about what we think we want? Do we see the whole picture or just a piece of it? Do our daydreams match our goals?

Actions we take today affect how we live tomorrow. If we know what we want—if we listen to our heart's desire, write down our goals, and keep them in mind with every action we take—we create our dreams. We turn our wishes into goals and our goals into reality.

Today I will visualize the life I want.

✦ ✦ ✦

June 1

Live out of your imagination, not your history.
—STEPHEN COVEY

◆　◆　◆

We may have never seen ourselves as having the potential to bring abundance into our lives. We've always assumed we'd make only a certain amount of money or always live in a starter house. We may not have even given much thought to how much money we could earn or to what our dream house would look like. If thoughts like these do pop into our heads, we dismiss them, thinking we don't have a chance.

We do have a chance. We just need to know in our heads what it is we really want. Then we have to know in our hearts. We have to feel it. We can visualize ourselves in a certain career, keep a scrapbook of pictures from magazine ads that depict interior designs we admire, or do a parade of homes tour. Then, we just have to believe, believe, believe.

Today I will, through my imagination, experience the life I want.

◆　◆　◆

June 2

The art of progress is to preserve order amid change
and to preserve change amid order.

—ALFRED NORTH WHITEHEAD

◆ ◆ ◆

We're finally making progress. We still have a lot of debt to pay off, but the feelings surrounding our debt have dissipated. We're out of the chaos and into the clarity. When we stop to think about it, we no longer mind being in debt.

At this stage, we discover that what bothered us most about being in debt was the loss of control; the going nowhere fast. When we have a firm understanding of what we've done and of what we can do to improve our situation, debt becomes just another part of life. We accept it. We don't fight it. We stop blaming ourselves or others. We simply handle our finances. We have time and energy to enjoy our lives. We may not be rich, but we're making progress. This alone is more gratifying than we could have imagined.

Today I will revel in my progress.

◆ ◆ ◆

June 3

Sympathy is a heart that understands.
—VICTOR ROBERTSON

◆   ◆   ◆

We're all unique in some way; we all lead different lives. We've all had our own set of experiences, the tally of which is ours and ours alone. As a result, we're sure no one will understand *our* situation. *No one* will understand. Why should we bother talking about it? If people don't understand, they won't be compassionate. They'll judge us or our loved one. We'll figure it out ourselves.

We're unique on one level, but we share common emotions and thoughts. While some people may not understand, plenty of people do. Many people have been there. We accept that the *main* reason we haven't told others about our money problems is that we don't want to air our dirty laundry. We want to continue to look good on the surface, while we struggle underneath.

**Today I will accept that unless I
seek support, the problems related to
my debt will only get worse.**

◆   ◆   ◆

June 4

Trouble is part of your life, and if you don't share it,
you don't give the person who loves you a chance
to love you enough.

—DINAH SHORE

◆ ◆ ◆

Some of us are not in the habit of asking for what we
need or of talking about our troubles. It makes us
feel uncomfortable. We don't want to be a bother. We
don't want to sound as if we're complaining all the time.
We feel we need to be strong.

Most people love to help. In the end, it makes them
feel loved, needed, and just plain good about themselves. We take the leap. We "try it on." We make some
mistakes—maybe talk too much to the wrong person or
don't say exactly what we need to say. Maybe we talk
when we really need quiet time. Over time, we figure
out who gives us the best feedback, who the best listeners are, and when is the best time to talk. It's trial
and error.

Today I will first listen to how I feel inside.
If I'm struggling, I share my thoughts with
a trusted confidant.

◆ ◆ ◆

June 5

When you are getting kicked from the rear,
it means you're in front.

—FULTON J. SHEEN

◆ ◆ ◆

Some people are great at speaking their minds. When we find someone we can trust to give us honest and direct feedback, we need to be ready to accept what they have to say. Often, the more honest and right on the feedback, the harder it is to take. We may even be angry at the messenger, blaming him or her for being too harsh.

Some information is hard to hear. The facts exist. We can't change the facts. What counts is how we react to what a supportive person tells us about the facts. We may need time to absorb the message. If the information is hard to take, we can bet that our support person has planted a seed that needs to sprout. We take time to dwell over the advice, to water that seed. When the time is right, we'll understand and accept the honest truth.

Today I will be open to hearing what supportive people have to say about my situation.

◆ ◆ ◆

June 6

Why wait any longer for the world to begin?
—PAUL WILLIAMS

◆　◆　◆

When our money problems leave us dazed and confused, how are we able to think clearly enough to take the first step toward getting the help we need? How do we even figure out what that step is?

We find one person we can trust. We begin by telling him or her as much as we're able to at the time. Maybe we say we're having some problems managing our money and are looking for help. We may confide in our friend about the source of our money problems, whether it be gambling, compulsive spending, or alcohol and drug dependency.

If we're still not at a point where we can talk honestly with supportive friends, we look in the phone book for hotlines (under Gambling, Alcoholics Anonymous, or Narcotics Anonymous). We talk but remain anonymous. If we're afraid our spouse will be angry with us, we ask that information be sent to our workplace or to a friend's house.

Today I will trust that the first step toward getting help is the hardest and that the process will get easier over time.

◆　◆　◆

June 7

I am an old man, and I have known a great many problems in my life, most of which never happened.

—MARK TWAIN

◆ ◆ ◆

Many of us spend a great deal of time worrying about problems that never transpire. We create "what if" scenarios, anticipate what could go wrong, and create an incredible amount of anxiety and possibly ill health and temper over something that never happens.

Anticipating what could go wrong and preparing ourselves to deal with it is wise planning. Creating obstacles and spending our days and nights worrying about them takes us off track.

Our mind-set becomes, "I can overcome." We immediately discard destructive thoughts and intentionally replace them with constructive thoughts.

Today I will act as if there are no obstacles.

◆ ◆ ◆

June 8

The best way to escape from a problem is to solve it.
—ALAN SAPORTA

♦ ♦ ♦

We all have desires and a need to be fulfilled. Following our worthy dreams is a way of nourishing our soul, of becoming whole. At times we may feel limited, believing we can't follow our dreams because we don't have the money.

We remind ourselves that we always have within us the stuff it takes to create a fulfilling life. Feeling trapped is a sign that we need to get creative. Imagination breaks through barriers.

Today I will reflect on what my true and deep desires are. I will use my imagination to discover opportunities that will help me fulfill my dreams and desires.

♦ ♦ ♦

June 9

Forget regret, or life is yours to miss.

—JONATHAN LARSON

◆　◆　◆

We dream about the past and wish life could be as it were before we married a gambler or an addict, before we started spending compulsively, before we or a loved one became chronically ill, before a divorce, when we had enough money to buy anything we wanted, or in a time when society was far less materialistic.

Memory, in addition to containing a fair amount of fiction, is selective. We think it through, and we see the negative, too. We stop wishing life could be as it was, and we empower ourselves to face current challenges, to enjoy today, and to move on.

Today I will be grateful for the new beginning that I am experiencing.

◆　◆　◆

June 10

Have courage to act instead of react.
—EARLENE LARSON JENKE

❖   ❖   ❖

Our behavior is sometimes a reflection of what kind of day we're having and vice versa. We may be treated poorly by our boss. Consequently, when we get home we yell at the kids. Or we may get frustrated and yell at our spouse for all the debt he's accrued, only to be reprimanded a little later for something we mishandled.

When we act with integrity, honesty, and kindness, we will encounter the same. Unexpectedly perhaps, we will see positive by-products—better relationships and health, the good things in life.

Today I will trust that living honestly puts me in the best position to receive the fruits of life.

❖   ❖   ❖

June 11

Money has never done a thing to anyone, never hurt a fly. Money is just money. But it is the power you give your money, or your attitudes toward and your fears about your money, that can wreak havoc on the most important relationships in your life.

—SUZE ORMAN

◆ ◆ ◆

Whether we want to focus on money or not and whether we're deep in debt or have money to burn, we need to share our thoughts and feelings about money with the people who are affected by our money decisions. We can't assume that our loved ones know and understand our thinking.

We realize that our feelings and attitudes about money affect those around us. Our feelings may be fear, anxiety, manipulation, or neediness. Our attitude toward money may drive us to hoard, spend, or control. By assuming we're entitled to feel and behave as we please with an object (money) that is an integral part of living with others—of our relationship with others— we risk damaging the relationships that count the most.

Today I will stop blaming money itself for my relationship problems and will talk about my feelings and attitudes about money with all involved.

◆ ◆ ◆

June 12

Pain is short, and joy is eternal.
—FRIEDRICH SCHILLER

◆　◆　◆

We feel ashamed of ourselves for having a large amount of consumer debt. We're embarrassed. We think others will see us as idiots who haven't figured out some of life's basic skills. If our spouses or children created the debt, we still have shame. We assume some of the responsibility.

When feelings of shame overwhelm us, the tendency is to want to withdraw, to isolate. We know that others will pick up on our feelings. We don't want to give them any clues. We don't want to embarrass ourselves further. We believe no one will understand. We choose to hide ourselves so we can hide the circumstances, thereby hiding the shame.

We consider that we are not alone. Millions of people are in over their heads, have addictions, are codependent, and feel what we're feeling. That means there are millions of people who can help us!

Today I will talk about my shame with one or two trustworthy people.

◆　◆　◆

June 13

God hasn't called me to be successful.
He's called me to be faithful.

—MOTHER TERESA

◆　◆　◆

Like addiction, debt knows no social boundaries. It afflicts the poor and the rich, clerks and doctors, janitors and famous entertainers. We'd like to think we're in debt because we don't make enough money and because the cost of living keeps rising. This is true for many of us, but some of us are in debt because we don't live within our means.

If we're in debt and in law school, we may still have the same money challenges when we're in our practice. As we work our way up the ladder, our money problems could climb up with us. Until we address our behaviors, get to the bottom of our thoughts, and work on our spirituality, our spending patterns will stay the same, regardless of our changing titles, positions, and income.

Today I will look at the real cause of my debt.

◆　◆　◆

June 14

Most people use God like a cow—for
the milk and cheese He can produce.

—MEISTER ECKHART

❖ ❖ ❖

The alcoholic is familiar with the prayer (or bargain),
"God, please get me out of this one, and I'll never
drink again." The high roller can feel a deep connection to a Power Greater when the stakes are on the
table. The chronically ill pray for a miracle. Spouses
pray in desperation.

We all have needs. When our needs are strong and
feel out of reach, many of us decide to turn to prayer,
perhaps for the first time in years; maybe for the first
time in our life. When we use prayer to meet our needs,
we can witness results. But to really know our Higher
Power, to really feel the connection, we pray regularly
and do not always have specific requests. In this way,
we receive what is our highest good.

Today I will pray with my heart, not my mind.

❖ ❖ ❖

June 15

For a quick refresher, erase the clutter from your mind.
—ANONYMOUS

♦ ♦ ♦

Studies have shown that prayer lowers stress levels and can heal disease (and heartache). Many of us don't need studies to believe in the miracle of prayer. We've experienced or witnessed its effectiveness.

Prayer is available to each and every one of us, regardless of whether we believe in a God (Buddhists, for example, pray as a way of life but not to a God-like figure) and regardless of how strong or nonexistent our faith. Prayer is available to us any time. Furthermore, it's free, and we cannot put a price tag on the benefits.

Today I will say a prayer of gratitude.

♦ ♦ ♦

June 16

Set your expectations high; find men and women whose integrity and values you respect; get their agreement on a course of action; and give them your ultimate trust.

—JOHN FELLOWS AKERS

◆ ◆ ◆

Many of us can think of people who are financially successful, who we respect, and who have a healthy relationship with money. If we don't, we can select someone famous who we imagine handles money well. We observe how these people treat money. What are their healthy money behaviors? Are these people generous yet not wasteful? Do they give you the sense that they understand money management? Do they know where their dollars are? Do they take care of themselves? Of others? Would they settle for the wages we're earning?

We observe and imagine what it would feel like to be a successful money manager. We emulate the behaviors we respect and admire. We use these people—whether or not they're aware of it—as role models.

Today I will consider who could be my financial role models.

◆ ◆ ◆

June 17

We control fifty percent of a relationship.
We influence one hundred percent of it.

—BARBARA COLOROSE

◆ ◆ ◆

We've all been influenced by the way our parents or guardians looked at money. Some of us grew up in households where money was never discussed. Or we may have been constantly reminded that the family didn't have enough money while our parents argued over paying the bills. Money may have been a form of manipulation. Some of us were aware of family finances and taught how to handle money.

Whether we've adopted the exact same or polar opposite attitude about money, we realize that our money thoughts started in childhood. When we attempt to understand where our parents or guardians were coming from regarding money, we have a better sense of why we look at money the way we do.

Today I will recall childhood money memories and consider how they continue to influence me.

◆ ◆ ◆

June 18

All the animals except for man know that the principal business of life is to enjoy it.
—SAMUEL BUTLER

◆ ◆ ◆

We work hard, and we worry hard. We have days when we feel we just can't keep doing what we do. We burn out. Our mind and body decide one day it's time to quit. We slouch on the couch and wonder what to do.

What we do is nothing. We give ourselves a well-deserved break. If possible, we take time off work. We get a sitter. We take time for ourselves. We stop fighting. We surrender and let ourselves rest and rejuvenate.

Today I will allow myself some time off.

◆ ◆ ◆

June 19

When you undervalue what you do,
the world will undervalue what you are.
—SUZE ORMAN

◆ ◆ ◆

We work for less than what we feel is right, yet we stay where we are. The feelings are reinforced every day—feelings of never having enough, of just getting by, of not deserving more, and of being a victim. We think these thoughts; we feel these feelings; we live this life.

We start by expecting more. We tell ourselves we deserve more. After all, we're really good at what we do. We get feedback from others. What can we do to increase our income? Do we ask for a raise? Interview for other jobs? Change careers? Go to school? Become self-employed? In reviewing our situation, we plant the seeds of change, abundance, and greater self-worth.

Today I will repeatedly tell myself I am worthy.

◆ ◆ ◆

June 20

Marriage is a two-handed game of solitaire.
—ANONYMOUS

◆　◆　◆

Being in charge of our own money is one thing. If we marry, finances are united, usually, at least to some extent. Although some couples keep their money separate, overlap exists. If our spouse, for instance, is deeply in debt and we want to go on vacation as a couple, what are our choices? If we're content to stay in the small, charming house we've nearly paid off but our new spouse falls in love with a four-storied Victorian that needs restoration, where do we draw the line?

We do not need to look back on any choices we've already made. We're where we are financially for better or for worse, so to speak. We communicate with our spouse not just about debt but about what we've learned about our own and our spouse's relationship with money. We don't need to tell our spouse everything he or she has done wrong, but we do need to recognize our needs. We communicate our needs honestly and directly, without arguing.

Today I will contemplate what I need from my spouse regarding money and spending.

◆　◆　◆

June 21

Learning to trust is one of life's most difficult tasks.

—ISAAC WATTS

◆　◆　◆

We marry for better or for worse, we expect some ups and downs, but once we feel we've been betrayed, we are lost.

If we've been lied to so many times we can no longer think straight, if we've been fooled into thinking we are at fault for an impossible financial situation because we don't work, don't earn enough, or because we spend too much, if we've been manipulated into believing that by co-signing a loan all our problems would disappear, or if our spouse has credit card bills delivered to a post office box or to another address, we've been betrayed. The person we thought we were supposed to trust and to turn to for emotional support is not being trustworthy or supportive.

Getting through betrayal is a long process, one that both parties must be willing to commit to in the most profound way. If one party is unwilling to be consistently trustworthy and the other is unwilling to forgive, the cracked foundation only crumbles further.

Today I will understand that trust is a core component of any successful relationship, and I will know that I deserve a trustworthy partner.

◆　◆　◆

June 22

We learn as much from sorrow as from joy,
as much from illness as from health, from handicap
as from advantage—and indeed perhaps more.

—PEARL S. BUCK

◆　◆　◆

If we or a loved one is suffering with a chronic or terminal illness or laid up from an accident, we may be
out of work either because we ourselves are sick or
because we need to function as caretaker. In addition
to losing income, we're confronted by a stream of medical bills not covered by insurance. We may already feel
completely overwhelmed by the illness or tragedy. How
do we face the debt, too?

If we're emotionally overwrought because of a
tragedy, we remember that the medical bills will wait.
We have a responsibility to deal with them somehow,
but our first responsibility is toward ourselves and to
whomever is ill. We can only handle so much at a time.
We allow ourselves to deal with our relationships and
our grief.

Today I will live one day at a time.

◆　◆　◆

June 23

Blessed is he who has learned to admire but not envy,
to follow but not imitate, to praise but not flatter,
and to lead but not manipulate.

—WILLIAM ARTHUR WARD

◆ ◆ ◆

Manipulation is not foreign to most of us. We have probably manipulated and been manipulated. Manipulators may or may not be aware of what they're doing. There may be no malice involved. Often, the only intention is to find the means to continue an addictive behavior. Manipulation, however, can be terrifying if we're the end receiver. We may also deny that it's happening, usually because we're so confused by it all. But when we realize the truth, we're frightened not only by what's happened, but also by what could happen. We've fallen for this before, what's to prevent us from falling for it again?

We do our best to detach from the manipulator. This may mean letting go physically, emotionally, spiritually, and mentally. The more distance we have, the easier it is to see the truth, to recognize the manipulation. When we must have contact, we keep our head on straight. If our former spouse calls us asking for money that he says is due to him, we give ourselves time to think. We don't need to answer to anyone right away. As time goes on, we're better able to identify and to deal appropriately with manipulative behavior.

Today I will have the courage to own the truth.

◆ ◆ ◆

June 24

What would it be like if you lived each day,
each breath, as a work of art in progress? Imagine that
you are a masterpiece unfolding, every second of
every day, a work of art taking form with every breath.

—THOMAS CRUM

◆　◆　◆

So many of us avoid living in the present moment. We regret getting into debt and worry about how our debt affects our future.

Daydreaming and pondering are necessary in moderation, but we try to stay in the present moment for most of the day. To do this, we return to the most basic element—our breath. We concentrate on taking deep breaths. Barring a respiratory disorder, breathing is simple. When we return to the simplicity of breathing, we automatically simplify our life by focusing only on what's happening to one part of our body in one moment in time.

**Today, when I have trouble living in the present,
I will concentrate on my breathing.**

◆　◆　◆

June 25

Minds are like parachutes; they work best when open.
—LORD THOMAS DEWAR

◆ ◆ ◆

The term *addiction* is used to refer to a broad range of behaviors—drinking, drugging, gambling, and overeating, for example. Science has acknowledged that ingesting chemicals (alcohol and other drugs) over a period of time alters brain chemistry in some people, in effect programming the brain to need more and more drugs and alcohol to maintain a certain level of "feel-good" neurotransmitters, such as endorphins, serotonin, and dopamine.

We can understand, even prove, that people get addicted to chemical substances and even to food, such as wheat or sugar. But how do people get addicted to gambling, sex, or exercise? Can we really call it addiction? Aren't these moral or body-image issues? Aren't we in a sense letting people off the hook by labeling them addicts?

Addiction is behavior that individuals cannot control. Stopping an addiction is not as easy as flicking a light switch. Addicts experience preoccupation, loss of control, and denial. Compulsive gamblers, spenders, and sex addicts experience all three.

**Today I will keep an open mind
about how I view addiction.**

◆ ◆ ◆

June 26

Made a list of all persons we had harmed, and
became willing to make amends to them all.

Made direct amends to such people wherever possible,
except when to do so would injure them or others.

—STEPS EIGHT AND NINE
OF ALCOHOLICS ANONYMOUS

◆ ◆ ◆

Apologizing to others for hurting them or causing
them grief is a powerful step toward healing. We
shed our guilt and shame, freeing ourselves up to live
our lives wholly.

We make a list of people we've harmed, not only for
the debt we've incurred but for all wrongs we've committed. We apologize in person whenever possible.
Unless we feel our apologies will create more pain, we
don't worry about how people will react to us. Most
people, we find, are receptive. If they aren't, we know
we have at least opened our hearts.

**Today and from now on I will admit when
I am wrong and apologize on the spot.**

◆ ◆ ◆

June 27

> God's foremost rule of finance is: We own nothing.
> We are managers, not owners. Stewards, not
> landlords. Maintenance people, not proprietors.
> Our money is not ours; it is his.

> —MAX LUCADO

◆ ◆ ◆

Most of us believe that our home, our possessions, and our money are ours. We own them. If someone takes them from us, they've committed a crime. We feel violated.

When we look at our money and the other things in our lives as if we own them, we feel entitled. We bought them, we earned it—of course they're ours. But if we believe in a Higher Power, if we believe life can be orchestrated to meet our needs, we believe that our talent, our money, our possessions, and our relationships all come from a higher source. They were given to us—and they can be taken away.

We can look at everything in our lives as if it were on loan. We're entitled to it only for as long as our Higher Power believes we need it. Our attitude then changes from one of entitlement to one of gratitude. Rather than cling to what we feel is rightfully ours, we let go. We feel the grace and serenity.

**Today I will view everything in my life
as if it were on loan.**

◆ ◆ ◆

June 28

Have patience with all things
but first of all with yourself.
—SAINT FRANCIS DE SALES

❖　❖　❖

When it comes to changing old behaviors, we get anxious. We're not that disciplined. It'll be hard. What will keep us motivated? We project into the future and, by doing so, convince ourselves we'll never be able to follow through for the rest of our lives. We can, however, do almost anything for twenty-four hours.

We choose to live one day at a time. We decide that for today, just today, we are not going to debt. No credit cards; no loans. We may panic. We start thinking about promises we made to go out, about dental work that needs to be done, and about past due bills, or we have an urge to drive to the casino or the mall. We relax and remember: One day at a time. As we stop debting, one day at a time, we affirm that we are capable of not getting deeper into debt. We gain serenity. When we're serene, we're better able to create solutions to our problems.

**Today—for the next twenty-four hours—
I will not use credit.**

❖　❖　❖

June 29

Let go and let God.

—ALCOHOLICS ANONYMOUS SLOGAN

◆　◆　◆

Letting go of worries and resentments that dominate our thoughts can seem impossible at times. We know we need to do it, but we don't know what to do. Nothing we read or tell ourselves seems to work.

When we can't let go emotionally or mentally, we try letting go physically. We find a box, a nice box, and designate it the God Box. We write down what's troubling us on a small piece of paper, put the paper in the box, close the lid, and forget about it. For now, it's in our Higher Power's hands. Later, we can just discard the contents of the box.

Today I will make a God (or Higher Power) Box.

◆　◆　◆

June 30

In a dark time, the eye begins to see.
—THEODORE ROETHKE

◆ ◆ ◆

Until we know what the problem is, we can't even begin to find a solution. Accepting that our debt has made our lives miserable and that we are responsible for our debt is a huge step. Some of us refuse to take it. We're fearful of what lies ahead. If we face it, what will happen?

Accepting that we have a problem with debt is the first step out of misery and into serenity. Accepting that we are directly responsible for our debt puts us in a position to make the best decisions for ourselves. If we deny that the problem exists, it will only get worse. If we accept that the problem exists, we can take appropriate action.

**Today I will accept that to move forward
I have to leave some of the familiar behind.**

◆ ◆ ◆

July 1

Adventure is the champagne of life.
—G. K. CHESTERTON

❖ ❖ ❖

Even with all there is to do in the world, with all the choices we have, we sometimes fall into the trap of being bored! We feel disconnected from others and not a part of the flow. We start to get depressed or to deepen a depression. Nothing much worthwhile seems to be happening to us. We hang around, waiting for something exciting to take place.

Boredom is often a sign that we're avoiding a feeling or not doing something that we're supposed to be doing. The feeling could be fear or loneliness. The task could be as simple as phoning the bank or facing bills or a family member. We put it off because we say we don't feel like doing it or the time isn't right.

Boredom is a sign that the time is right—overdue, in fact. We may have a fear or two behind our inaction. We face our feelings, tackle the project, get back into the flow—we seek the adventure.

**Today I will approach boldly the tasks
I've been putting off.**

❖ ❖ ❖

July 2

Change is not merely necessary to life. It is life.
—ALVIN TOFFLER

◆　◆　◆

Routine and healthy habits serve us well. They help us get through the day with little thought and energy. If we're on a spending plan and have to discipline ourselves not to spend money in certain categories, we may start to feel as if life has become too predictable. Too much routine makes us feel listless. We have our goals and our priorities, but even working toward our dreams starts to tire us.

When we're on the verge of feeling like all this planning is too much, too boring, too unlike us, we put our egos in check by throwing in something new. It doesn't have to be grandiose. In fact, the simpler the better. We think of activities that we never thought we'd do, and we do them. Have we ever gone swing dancing? Made a banana cream pie? Gone skinny-dipping?

**Today I will do (or plan to do)
one thing I've never done before.**

◆　◆　◆

July 3

As he thinketh in his heart, so is he.

—PROVERBS 23:7

◆　◆　◆

How we view our circumstances directly affects how we feel about them. Being in debt can cause us to cast dark shadows over our world, shadows that create a sense of doom and gloom. "I can't get out from under it"; "I can't go on vacation"; "I can't get my hair cut, buy a shirt, go out to dinner, get season tickets"; "I would go to school but . . . "

Most of us were told as children not to say "can't" and to "never say never." We rephrase our negative thoughts and statements in the positive and in the present, as if the positive already exists. Our outlook and, amazingly, our circumstances brighten considerably. Ideas about how to move forward pop into our head, replacing excuses with a powerful energy—an energy that moves us toward accomplishing our goals.

Today I will ask myself whether I see the glass as half empty or half full.

◆　◆　◆

July 4

Money brings some happiness. But after
a certain point, it just brings more money.

—NEIL SIMON

◆　◆　◆

We've stopped debting, and we're paying off our
credit cards, one by one. We have a strong sense
of purpose, and we know what we value. One day, we'll
come out ahead. We'll start saving and investing. We'll
feel relieved, proud, and happy. Some of the happiness
derives from having money, but much of it is from
achieving what we set out to do—for affirming that we
can do what we say we're going to do.

While the joy that comes with being debt-free may
never wane, the thrill of having money does. The
money we have just brings in more money. That's it.
But what we do with our money, our lifestyle, our relationships today determines the quality of our life and
our level of abundance tomorrow.

**Today I will know that with my financial
independence come greater responsibilities.**

◆　◆　◆

July 5

No man can think clearly when his fists are clenched.

—GEORGE JEAN NATHAN

◆　◆　◆

We know the feeling. Our muscles tighten. Our minds begin to race with thoughts of all our problems. We feel incredibly overwhelmed, helpless, and fearful. The sense that something tragic will overtake our lives is powerful. Some of us may feel suicidal during these periods.

When we're feeling anxious, we do our best to relax. We take deep breaths, take a hot bath or shower, go for a long walk, get a massage—whatever works. We then do something to attack at least one of the problems spiraling out of control in our head. We acknowledge that the others will have to wait. We relax our bodies; we calm our minds. The anxiety dissipates. In a relaxed state, we are better able to approach the other problems on our minds.

**Today I will write down three action steps
I can take toward solving one problem.**

◆　◆　◆

July 6

I asked God for new eyes and ears.
—ELEANOR K.

◆ ◆ ◆

Addiction is so prevalent that it may be safe to say that nearly everybody knows at least one addict—a drug addict, alcoholic, gambler, sex addict, compulsive spender, or overeater. Accepting that we or someone we care about is an addict begins with being able to identify some of the telltale signs, the addictive behaviors.

To be able to adapt to the addictive lifestyle, addicts take on certain behaviors. Behaviors common to addicts include betrayal (of self and others), lying, blaming, and withdrawing or isolating. Addicts also create rituals around their addiction: wearing the same "winning" shirt to the casino, pulling the blinds down before using, popping breath mints before leaving the bar. Each time an addict rationalizes or denies an addictive behavior, they make a commitment to their addiction; they give it strength.

Today I will gain strength by encouraging awareness in myself and others.

◆ ◆ ◆

July 7

Fear is the main source of superstition,
and one of the main sources of cruelty.
To conquer fear is the beginning of wisdom.

—BERTRAND RUSSELL

◆ ◆ ◆

The fear of rejection keeps some of us from achieving all sorts of goals—from getting a new and better job to creating fulfilling relationships. We take outcomes personally—we didn't get the job because they didn't like us, or we weren't good enough. We focus on the negative, hurtful aspects. In truth, we probably didn't get the job because someone else was simply a better fit for the company. The decision had nothing to do with us.

We consider what we tend to have negative, self-defeating thoughts about. *Why can't I get a better job? How come nobody calls me? Why won't the bank give me a loan?* Then we reverse the thoughts. *How do I get a better job? Who can I call? How can I get my finances in good enough shape for a loan?* We take action. If we're rejected, we don't take it personally. We change the game plan. We persist long enough to get beyond our fear of rejection.

Today I will take initiative.

◆ ◆ ◆

July 8

Visualize your hands placing in God's hands the person
or problem you are concerned about. Visualize
His hands gently and lovingly holding that person or
willingly accepting that problem. Now, visualize His
hands holding you. All is well for the moment.

—MELODY BEATTIE

♦ ♦ ♦

Our spouse, siblings, or parents are gambling or spending compulsively. We're always bailing them out. We're angry. Don't they know what they're doing? We yell, nag, and cry in our attempts to control their behavior. We have an intense need to set things straight, but the situation only deteriorates.

We are tormented by a seemingly hopeless situation that we refuse to give up on. We're on the verge of a nervous breakdown, and we're not even the source of the trouble!

We may not be the source of the compulsive behavior, but we do need to look at our behavior. We're trying to control someone. Addiction does not respond to yelling, nagging, and crying. An addict does not heal through our codependency. In fact, our codependency actually prevents progress. We let go of the need to control. We visualize handing the problem over to our Higher Power. We sit back, take a deep breath, and begin healing ourselves.

Today I will begin my healing process.

♦ ♦ ♦

July 9

The brighter you are, the more you have to learn.
—DON HEROLD

◆ ◆ ◆

We get an idea about how to make money fast. Our heart begins to pound, we start to perspire, and we can't wait to talk about it with our friends. Our adrenaline rises. This feels right. We know this is it— this is the scheme that will get us out of debt. We'll be rich. We'll have found the Big Fix.

We slow down and get centered. We recall past schemes that have failed and remember the shame and despair that followed. Get-rich schemes work for some people, but they haven't worked for us. And if by chance they did, we'd find ourselves deep in debt again. If we don't change our money behaviors, we'll go back to square one.

Today I will accept that the instant gratification route always leads me back to where I started.

◆ ◆ ◆

July 10

Wisdom enables one to be thrifty without being
stingy and generous without being wasteful.

—UNKNOWN

◆　◆　◆

We know when we're being cheap, we know when
we're being overly generous, and we know when
we're being wasteful. We're conscious, and, for the most
part, we know when we're guilty of acting a certain way,
even though we may not admit it to ourselves or others.

We need to reach a middle ground—the amount of
spending and saving that's right for us. Not everyone
has the same middle ground; no one can tell us where
that is. We know it when we feel it.

**Today I will discern when I'm spending too much
or too little and will correct my behavior the
next time. In doing so, I find balance.**

◆　◆　◆

July 11

The universe is full of magical things,
patiently waiting for our wits to grow sharper.
—EDEN PHILLPOTTS

◆　◆　◆

We hear others talk about how they got out of debt. We see people who have peace and serenity in their lives, who have healthy relationships and dream jobs. We realize that being debt-free means more than not having to pay as many bills. In others, we see what we have to look forward to by changing our behaviors. We get inspired and excited to be debt-free. We start working the program diligently, expecting to see miracles in our lives any minute . . . but nothing happens.

We stop focusing on the outcome of our new ways and stay mindful of what we've committed to—no debting one day at a time. When we do this, we give energy to everything good. If we stop focusing on it, it will flow to us.

Today I will trust that when I act in a mindful and honorable way, everything good will follow.

◆　◆　◆

July 12

He who receives a benefit with gratitude
repays the first installment on his debt.

—SENECA

◆ ◆ ◆

While we're in the midst of our debt, our perceived
poverty, we may get so low we forget to be grateful for what we have. But when things start to look up
for us, we may look back and remember only what we
had to be grateful for—the good things about our debting days.

Being in debt does not have to be the worst time of
our lives. There's much to be grateful for—always. As
much as debt creates stress, it can also heighten other
aspects of our lives. We may not be able to go out to
restaurants often or take a dream cruise, but we've got
our children, our friends, and our family. We're learning new values. We're learning about ourselves.

**Today I will appreciate what being
in debt has brought to my life.**

◆ ◆ ◆

July 13

God, grant me the serenity
To accept the things I cannot change,
The courage to change the things I can,
And the wisdom to know the difference.

—REINHOLD NIEBUHR

◆ ◆ ◆

The Serenity Prayer tells us to let go of what we can't change and to change what we can. What if we don't have the wisdom to know the difference? What then?

One way to acquire wisdom is to learn from our mistakes and our victories. We learn to take positive action to improve our situation. We may, for instance, not know whether we can convince our spouse to stop spending compulsively. We reason, plead, kick, and holler, but nothing changes. We've taken our action. It didn't work. We learned we can't change our spouse. We let go of that option.

We look for another variable. What else can we change? Our behavior? Our living situation? Our accounts? Can we take some legal action to protect our finances? Even though our first action didn't work, it moved us forward. We're now ready to try something else.

Today I will be wise enough to know that just taking action is success in and of itself.

◆ ◆ ◆

July 14

Knowledge is power.
—FRANCIS BACON

◆　◆　◆

Most of us don't just want to get out of debt. We want it with a passion. We want it so bad it hurts.

We take advantage of the passion. We read whatever books we can find on getting out of debt, on living simply, and on cutting costs. We compare what the experts have to say. We learn everything we can, and we learn it well. We tell others what we've learned. We apply what we've learned until getting out of debt becomes so natural we don't know how we could live any other way but debt-free.

Today I will know the basic steps for getting out of debt like I know the back of my hand.

◆　◆　◆

July 15

Diamonds are nothing more than
chunks of coal that stuck to their jobs.

—MALCOLM FORBES

◆　◆　◆

When we value something deeply, we strongly hold onto our beliefs about it. If we value money, for instance, we believe that we should not be wasteful with it. If we value our car, we believe in changing the oil and getting tune-ups regularly. If we value a friendship, we believe it's important to call and to keep our promises. We do what we say we're going to do and what we believe is right. And we do it consistently.

We give strength to what we value because we firmly *believe* in it. We apply the same type of tenacity to getting out of debt. We make getting out of debt something we value. In doing so, any actions we take to get out of debt are upheld by the power of our beliefs. With this strength, we are able to persistently and consistently turn our debt into diamonds.

**Today I will see myself as being
tenacious about living a debt-free life.**

◆　◆　◆

July 16

Assumptions allow the best in life to pass you by.
—JOHN SALES

◆ ◆ ◆

Everyone makes mistakes, and we can be sure that the credit card companies and banks we work with are no exception.

We need to be religious about reviewing our credit card statements every month. We can't afford not to. We check that our payment has been recorded and whether a late charge has been added. We also double-check the interest rate we're being charged. Are we actually getting the low introductory rate we were promised? Has the interest rate mysteriously gone up? Was our transfer put in the purchases category rather than in the lower-interest-rate transferred balances category?

If we find a mistake, we don't need to get angry. We calmly call the company responsible and politely but firmly inform them of the mistake. We request that we be reimbursed for any extra interest we've paid.

**Today I will not take for granted
that all business is taken care of.**

◆ ◆ ◆

July 17

Many of us love but don't have
a clue about what a healthy relationship is.

—EARNIE LARSEN

◆　◆　◆

Relationships involve more than love. They involve skill. We need to know how to communicate, listen, give, take, and let go. We may have found the love of our life, but if we don't have solid relationship skills, our marriage may end up as another divorce statistic.

Money management is an important relationship skill. When we're open with our partner about our feelings and intentions with money, when we're aware of our spending patterns and talk them through, when we're honest and willing to see our faults and strengths, we put ourselves in a healthy position financially—and romantically. There are no secrets, so our partner won't feel betrayed or deceived. We expect the same from our partner. We work together.

**Today I will treat my partner
the way I would like to be treated.**

◆　◆　◆

July 18

Home life ceases to be free and beautiful
as soon as it is founded on borrowing and debt.
—HENRIK IBSEN

◆ ◆ ◆

Money is a leading cause of disagreements among couples. One partner wants to take out a home improvement loan while the other wants to save the money for the project first. One partner wants to invest and the other wants to pay off credit card debt. We may voice our concerns about getting into debt only to be told everything will be fine.

Once debt starts to accumulate, it can easily spiral out of control. We're wise to question unplanned expenses or poor money management. Charging new kitchen cabinets and a new floor may be enough to put us under. To get by, we may have to start charging for necessities such as gasoline or groceries. When we invest our money before we've paid off credit card debt, we're thinking about our future without regard for the present. If our investments go bad and we've accumulated debt, we've created a double jeopardy.

When we're concerned about our partner's money behaviors, we do more than express our concerns. We lay it on the line. We document the debts, and we record expenses daily. We show our partner on paper what's happening. We give concrete evidence. Rather than argue, we negotiate a plan.

Today I will back up my concerns with evidence.

◆ ◆ ◆

July 19

Humor is an affirmation of man's dignity, a declaration
of man's superiority to all that befalls him.
—ROMAIN GARY

◆　◆　◆

Sometimes—at a funeral, for instance—we catch ourselves laughing when we think we should be crying.
Both laughter and tears can provide a catharsis. They
relieve stress and tension. While laughter is sometimes
inappropriate, it's often the best cure.

Being able to laugh at ourselves is one of our greatest gifts. It puts us above the emotional drudgery. It
shows dignity and true perspective. We cannot change
what has happened to us; we can only change how we
react to it.

Today I will laugh.

◆　◆　◆

July 20

The Constitution only gives people the right to
pursue happiness. You have to catch it yourself.

—BEN FRANKLIN

◆ ◆ ◆

We're feeling good as we get our life in order.
We've stopped incurring unsecured debt, we've
faced our addiction, or maybe we've divorced an
addicted spouse. We're making progress—and then we
start to feel guilty. Guilty for doing well and for getting
ahead while people we know are still in dire straits. How
can we feel so good when others are still suffering?
Shouldn't we be helping them? To escape this kind of
guilt, we may even be tempted to jump back down into
the muck and start debting again.

We acknowledge that while we can try to help those
still in need by being there for them, we are not responsible for turning their lives around. We can give healthy
support, but we are not responsible for their debt or
addiction. Only they can make the leap.

Today I will know that I sometimes
help people best by letting them be.

◆ ◆ ◆

July 21

It is very iniquitous to make me pay my debts;
you have no idea of the pain it gives one.
—LORD BYRON

◆　◆　◆

It can hurt to sit down and pay the bills. Every time we write out a check to cover gambling debts or the disastrous result of a get-rich scheme, anger wells up inside us. If we did not incur the debt ourselves, we may feel powerless. We had no control over how much of our money was lost—wasted. Worse yet, we have no control over what will happen today, tomorrow, or the next day.

We tell ourselves we can't just detach or let go, because the situation will only get worse. We have to be on guard and as knowledgeable as we can. But no matter how many trips we make to the casino to catch our partner there, no matter how much we yell and complain about the size of the debt—no matter what we do or say—the debt rises. The debt is still out of control, and we pay for it with our money and our peace of mind.

When we let go of our attachment to wishing our loved ones would behave as we want them to, we act from a state of serenity rather than rage. We save our sanity. In a sane state, we can create solutions.

Today I will strive for serenity first.

◆　◆　◆

July 22

A car is an invention which makes
people go fast and money faster.
—Jimmy Lyons

◆　◆　◆

Cars are a common big-ticket item. Most of us have and need them. Many of us treat our cars as temporary. We have a plan to keep them for two, four, or five years and then to trade them in for a newer model. While we have them, some of us remember only to fill them with gas. We forget to change the oil regularly, we don't bother with tune-ups, we allow them to collect clutter and dust.

We remember that even though cars begin to depreciate as soon as we drive them off the lot, we spend a huge amount of money on our vehicles. The better we take care of them, the longer they'll last. The longer they last, the more time we have without car payments. What if we buy a car with the mind-set of keeping it for seven or ten years? How would we treat our cars then?

Today I will look at my car as an investment.

◆　◆　◆

July 23

You cannot cut down the tree that gives you shade.

—ARABIAN PROVERB

◆ ◆ ◆

Those of us addicted to one thing or another eventually discover that we're using substances (drugs, alcohol, money) or stimulating environments (casinos) to numb or escape some intense and painful feelings.

Another common denominator in addiction is a lack of spirituality. In numbing our feelings, we numb our spirits. We feel no connection to a Higher Power. We may have no desire to connect, or we may have faith that some day it will happen. We may even "see the light"—know that if we turn a certain way we can have what we seek—but we're so afraid that when we turn to the light and the truth is revealed, we will be overwhelmed with pain.

Our Higher Power, our spirituality, is the tree that gives us shelter. If we cut down that tree—cut off our connection to a Power greater than ourselves—we are lost and vulnerable to the elements.

**Today I will see my Higher Power
as a tremendous source of healing.**

◆ ◆ ◆

July 24

Vision is a waking dream.
—HENRY WADSWORTH LONGFELLOW

◆　◆　◆

We can't help but notice other families who seem to manage their money well, and we wonder how they do it. A young couple is buying a middle-class home. The family with three kids and a stay-at-home mom always has enough to take an annual vacation. They've given their money attention, they take care of their finances, and they reap the rewards.

By observing others, we realize that a life without unsecured debt and with the things we want is achievable. It takes discipline, awareness, and a plan. We know that if others can do it, so can we.

Today I am inspired by the achievements of others.

◆　◆　◆

July 25

When we pray to God, we must
be seeking nothing—nothing.

—SAINT FRANCIS OF ASSISI

◆ ◆ ◆

We may have heard the Jewish proverb, "Do you know how to make God laugh? Show him your plans." If we believe we're here on earth for a reason, we believe that our Higher Power knows the reason. And, deep within, if we only listen, we'll know the reason, too.

One of the best ways to get the message is to ask our Higher Power how we can serve it. Maybe the answer comes to us through the people we meet or through a strong feeling. We stop praying to our Higher Power to solve all our problems and to make us happy. When our desire is to serve, our prayers are answered.

**Today and from now on I will end
every prayer with "Thy will be done."**

◆ ◆ ◆

July 26

Procrastination is a form of fear.

—DAVE KULSRUD

❖ ❖ ❖

Mail from collection agencies remains unopened. We let the phone ring until the answering machine picks it up for fear it's a creditor. If we do answer the phone, we may be so annoyed with the creditor that we yell and slam down the receiver.

As painful as it may be, as resentful or fearful as we may feel, we make it a point to communicate with our creditors honestly and openly. After all, when we (or whoever) started using our credit cards, we officially agreed to the terms. For whatever reason, we're the party at fault. It's our responsibility to do whatever is reasonable to fulfill our obligations to people and to companies.

Today I will remember that communicating with creditors is a form of making amends.

❖ ❖ ❖

July 27

It is better to die on your feet
than to live on your knees!
—EMILIANO ZAPATA

◆　◆　◆

Once we finally get a grip on how much money we need for basic expenses, we may be shocked to learn that we have little or nothing left to pay creditors. We'd been meeting our basic needs only by charging. We continued to charge, got deeper in debt, and were able to meet even fewer needs. The cycle continued until it finally spun out of control.

Our spending plan may need to include a debt moratorium. We may need to tell a creditor or two that we cannot pay anything for a specified period of time. We're firm and honest. We let them know our intentions are good. With good intentions, our actions are admirable. We are not neglecting a responsibility; we are working toward a solution.

**Today I will know that honorable
intentions lead toward solvency.**

◆　◆　◆

July 28

You're either part of the solution or part of the problem.
—ELDRIDGE CLEAVER

◆　◆　◆

Shame and fear may be keeping us isolated and secretive about our debt. When it comes time to break the cycle of debting, we need to replace destructive behaviors. We can rely on a support system whenever a new behavior seems too challenging.

Calling creditors, many of whom have been less than friendly, can be intimidating, especially if we don't think they're going to like what we have to say or if we don't know our legal rights. To meet this challenge, it's helpful to "bookend"—to call a support person before and after the action. We can talk about any fears or concerns before we call and process what happened afterward. With this type of support, we can get beyond our fears.

Today I will use my support system.

◆　◆　◆

July 29

Sympathy is an impulse toward ourselves
through the heart of another.
—ELBERT HUBBARD

◆　◆　◆

We want to make sure we choose the most appropriate people to help us while we change our behaviors. Not everyone has the right skills for the job. We need to figure out which people help us the most in which circumstances.

Initially, we may want to turn to friends and family we trust. We look for nonjudgmental, compassionate people who listen. We may choose to get help from someone who's not emotionally involved with us—a therapist, for instance. We also look for people who've had the same debting experiences as we've had. Many such people can be found at support group meetings such as Debtors Anonymous.

Today I will follow my intuition about people.

◆　◆　◆

July 30

Will is faith and persistency.
—ALDOUS HUXLEY

◆ ◆ ◆

We may not believe we have the strength, courage, and wisdom to change our behaviors. We may not know if what we want is really what's best for us and our family. We may not know if we really want to stop gambling, drinking, drugging, or spending compulsively. We may want nothing to do with self-help groups or with praying, meditating, and a Higher Power.

One thing we do know is that something has to change, and the only person we can change is ourself. When we become willing to change we take a big step forward. If we make our best effort—put forward as much time and energy to paying off our debt and to changing our behaviors as we did to our destructive behaviors—we'll see results.

Today I am willing to trust the process.

◆ ◆ ◆

July 31

We must hang together, gentlemen . . .
else, we shall most assuredly hang separately.

—BENJAMIN FRANKLIN

◆ ◆ ◆

Many of us were raised to be strong and independent. Our families gave us the skills we needed to be self-reliant. When our parents had a problem, they dealt with it—or kept it in the family, hidden from the rest of the world. Self-reliance can be a great asset, but some of us take it to an extreme. We associate seeking help from others with being weak.

Asking for help is something we need to "try on." We take small steps at first—maybe call a friend to talk about our debt. We go to a support group meeting. We don't have to like it at first, but we give it a chance. At some point, we'll be able to help others with the same issues we're struggling with now. Slowly, we begin to see that accepting and giving help is a way to bond, to strengthen relationships.

**Today I will accept help so that
I may be able to give help in the future.**

◆ ◆ ◆

August 1

Opportunity is making the most from one's resources.

—ANONYMOUS

◆　◆　◆

If we're at a point—or when we get to a point—where we get offers for low-interest-rate credit cards and are actually accepted, we need to take the time to take advantage of the opportunities. Even if the rate drops by only a percentage point or offers only a three- or six-month introductory rate, we can save hundreds of dollars a year in interest by taking the few minutes it takes to fill out the form or to call the company. Once the balance has been transferred, we immediately close the old account. In addition, we do not skip making a payment on the closed account. We add that money to the next payment.

This is no time for loyalty. We may have been with the same credit card company for years, but we need to have our best interests in mind—our financial future is at stake.

Today I will know that balance transfers are not a solution but an aid to help me decrease debt.

◆　◆　◆

August 2

Don't tell me I'm burning the candle at both ends—
tell me where I can get more wax.
—UNKNOWN

◆　◆　◆

We're exhilarated after we have our first big win at the casino; we feel euphoric when we drink our first beer; the adrenaline rushes through our veins as we near the clearance section. The feeling—the high—we get with these experiences is so incredible we want more. We want to recreate that feeling again and again. So we go back to the source, but find that the high is never quite the same as the first time. We chase the feeling, but we never catch up to it because we now need more than we did the first time.

Regardless, we believe we will catch it someday. Someday everything will be fine, we convince ourselves and others. Desperately chasing a feeling associated with gambling, drinking, drugging, or compulsive spending is a sign of addiction.

Today I will consider what it is I'm looking for.

◆　◆　◆

August 3

The biggest liar was my own addiction.
—JOANIE R.

◆　◆　◆

We may be in recovery, abstaining from addictive substances such as drugs or alcohol. One day a friend invites us to a casino to kill a few hours. We reason that the outing would be harmless enough. After all, we're alcoholics, not gamblers. We enjoy ourselves, blow the twenty dollars we'd planned to lose, and leave feeling as though we had control.

We had control. What a wonderful feeling. It's not like with drugs or alcohol, we tell ourselves. So we go back the next week and the next. We might even be winning enough to make ourselves feel as if we've taken on a second job—as if we're improving our financial situation. We look forward to our weekly visit to the casino with our friend. One night, we're feeling a bit on edge. We decide to go without our friend; we make an unscheduled visit. We're feeling down and so allow ourselves a bigger bankroll. Before we know it we're caught in the addictive cycle again, turning to gambling, instead of drugs, for our high or escape. We've replaced one addiction with another.

Today I will accept that my addictive personality
is vulnerable to all types of addictions,
and I will stay away from slippery places.

◆　◆　◆

August 4

Even in the common affairs of life, in love, friendship,
and marriage, how little security have we when
we trust our happiness in the hands of others!

—PAUL AUBUCHON

◆ ◆ ◆

We're sober now. We haven't been gambling. We haven't been to the mall. Why won't our spouses, parents, or friends trust us? Why won't they believe us when we say we're working late? Why are we being treated like children? We need support, not accusations!

We accept that we've been irresponsible with money and that as a result, we've hurt a lot of people. We've also lost a tremendous amount of trust. We've lied one too many times before; why should our loved ones believe us now that we're in recovery? We've made progress, but rebuilding trust takes time. We gracefully accept that we can't make others believe us, we can't change their feelings, and we can't avoid coming home late sometimes. We don't blame others for wrongly accusing us. We try to understand their point of view.

**Today I will know that if I stay on track,
I will earn the trust of others in time.**

◆ ◆ ◆

August 5

Love your suffering. Do not resist it,
do not flee from it. Give yourself to it.

—HERMANN HESSE

❖ ❖ ❖

Illness and addiction cause a great deal of pain. The
temptation is to resist the intense feelings. Many of
us fear that if we allow ourselves to go there, we won't
be strong enough to emerge. We bury the feelings or
numb them with drugs and alcohol or by gambling or
spending compulsively.

When we embrace rather than fight a feeling or a situation, we take a big step toward getting through it. For
those of us who've stuffed our feelings, the concept of
loving our suffering can seem unbearable. Yet in the
depth of our pain, we can be grateful that we are at least
feeling once again. Out of the pain comes growth and
joy.

**Today I will take comfort in knowing
that pain precedes growth.**

❖ ❖ ❖

August 6

We must embrace the absurd and
go beyond everything we have ever known.
—JANIE GUSTAFSON

◆　◆　◆

At some point in our life, we may have felt betrayed by our Higher Power and stopped caring whether it existed or not. Our faith may have ended as a child or just recently. Or maybe we were raised without religion or spirituality. We may feel clueless about believing in a Power greater than ourselves.

If we want to find spirituality but don't know how, we "act as if" we believe. We repeat a prescribed mantra. We try praying and meditating. We may want to attend church services. If we feel we can't get close to religion, we consider the Higher Power concept. If we're in a support group, we may try to start believing in a Power Greater by calling the group itself our Higher Power, referring to the positive, affirming, and motivating energy the group creates.

Today I will "act as if" I believe.

◆　◆　◆

August 7

It takes courage (and, perhaps, a leap of faith) to enter
into a financial free fall with someone else, trusting you
will be better off by relinquishing your money for the
sake of the greater good of your marriage.

—Suze Orman

◆　◆　◆

We bring our hearts and souls into a committed
relationship, but some of us are reluctant to
bring our checkbooks. If we're coming into a marriage
or partnership with a lot of debt, we can understand
our partner's reluctance. We haven't done very well
with our money thus far. How can we expect them to
trust us on that level?

We make financial commitments to ourself and
our partner. We take responsibility for the debt we enter
the relationship with. We also share household
expenses, each of us paying an equal percentage of our
income. This means that the one earning the most
money puts forward the most money. We unite our
financial goals. When the pot is bigger, financial goals
are more readily achieved.

**Today I will know that if I am committed
to paying my debt, I can expect my partner
to be committed to our financial future.**

◆　◆　◆

August 8

Money will buy a bed, but not sleep;
Books, but not brains;
Food, but not appetite;
Finery, but not beauty;
A house, but not a home;
Medicine, but not health;
Luxuries, but not culture;
Amusement, but not happiness;
Religion, but not salvation;
A passport to everywhere but heaven.

—UNKNOWN

◆ ◆ ◆

What do we expect will happen to us after we get our finances in order? Do we envision that because we'll be richer (that is, not in debt), we'll be happier, have better relationships, and find peace of mind?

All of the above is possible, but we remember that we achieve these goals not by having more money but by working on our behavior and our spirituality. We know that money and getting out of debt are not cure-alls. We'll still worry, get angry, get sad, and long for something more. That's life. We remember that the self-improvement process we use to get out of debt leaves us better equipped to handle life's problems.

Today I will know that the only price for serenity is having the courage to look within.

◆ ◆ ◆

August 9

He is rich who owes nothing.

—HUNGARIAN PROVERB

◆ ◆ ◆

If we're recording our expenses daily, placing them in categories, and working from a spending plan, we can actually feel like we're making conscious decisions about where our money needs to go. This is empowering and a great relief.

While we're keeping track of our expenses, we need to be sure we're not handing out more than we're getting in. If our expenses exceed our net income even by ten dollars, we're incurring new debt. We need to cut expenses in a category (or two) or find a way to bring in more money (sell something, take on extra projects).

Today I will remember that debting is not an option.

◆ ◆ ◆

August 10

The spirit is an inward flame; a lamp
the world blows upon but never puts out.

—MARGOT ASQUITH

◆　◆　◆

Focusing on the negative consequences of our debt is stressful. It leads to feelings of inadequacy. We can choose to focus our attention elsewhere—on our spirit.

When we feel hurt, down, and empty because of how we're being treated or because of our circumstances, we shift our attention inward. We ask our Higher Power to fill up the emptiness. We tell ourselves we're complete. When we focus on what we truly are, we can only focus on the positive. Instead of losing precious energy on the negative, we create energy in the positive.

Today I will allow myself to feel whole.

◆　◆　◆

August 11

Dealing with our emotions is much more difficult
than handling the economics because emotions are
subjective. . . . We can't put them on a spreadsheet and
move them around until they balance perfectly. We can't
project them the way we project income and expenses.

—MARY HUNT

◆ ◆ ◆

Even those of us who never made it beyond algebra
and who in our adult lives have avoided math like
the plague discover that personal finance is not rocket
science. We buy a book on money management and see
that it's really quite simple. We keep records. We add,
subtract, and sometimes divide. We learn we can handle the economics.

But what if we've got all the bookkeeping down pat
and still can't manage to live within our means? We look
to our emotions, the more complex aspect of our money
behaviors.

Today I will look for the true source of my debt.

◆ ◆ ◆

August 12

Is your cucumber bitter? Throw it away.
Are there briars in your path? Turn aside.
That is enough. Do not go on to say, Why were
things of this sort ever brought into the world?

—MARCUS AURELIUS

◆　◆　◆

Our debt has gotten so out of control that we're humiliated. Humiliated because the car is making noise, the deck is falling apart, and the house needs painting, but we can't afford to do anything about it. We live in a two-income family, and we bring in a lot of money every month; we should be able to afford a house on the Riviera. Yet we can't even pay our bills each month.

Feeling humiliated can make us feel enraged. We're embarrassed and we feel powerless. We blame our partner or ourselves. It also leads to isolation. The more humiliated we feel, the more we want to hide. If we go public, we think the humiliation will only escalate to unbearable levels.

We acknowledge that we're not the only people in debt and that it is not the end of the world. The longer we hide, the greater the chance that our debt will continue to increase. We open up and talk to others. By telling our secrets, our humiliation dies.

Today I will choose humility over humiliation.

◆　◆　◆

August 13

You shall know the truth, and
the truth shall make you mad.

—ALDOUS HUXLEY

◆　◆　◆

If we're living with someone who's addicted to gambling, drinking, or drugging, we've probably been lied
to frequently over the years. We may have been lied
to so much, in fact, that we feel we're going crazy. We're
told something one day and something different another day. When we question it, the addict denies saying
anything or tells us we misunderstood. We start to question our memories and become confused. We truly can't
remember what was said when. When this happens
repeatedly, our sense of reality goes out the door.

When an addict lies, it usually is not to be vindictive.
Lying is a way for addicts to stay in denial—a place they
need to stay if they are going to uphold their addiction.
Regardless, we need to protect ourselves from getting
serious misinformation about money and from going
insane. We learn to trust our memories again. We document, if necessary, conversations we've had about
mortgages or loans. We get information from outside
sources who can confirm or deny the "facts" given to
us by an addict.

**Today I will not be swayed
into mistrusting my memory.**

◆　◆　◆

August 14

We never know the worth of water till the well is dry.
—ENGLISH PROVERB

◆ ◆ ◆

We may believe that everything in our lives is wrong. We're deep in debt, our marriage is suffering because of it, and we have no idea how we're going to reach a resolution.

Our extremely adverse financial circumstances have actually given us a financial advantage over many other people. If the well is dry, and we're so very thirsty, how can that be to our advantage?

Our debt—our dry well—is our motivator and our teacher. We're being motivated, or maybe forced, to learn the value of money. We're also learning the rewards of responsibility and that when we're conscious of our choices, we can create the future we want.

Today I take advantage of my opportunities.

◆ ◆ ◆

August 15

A disciplined conscience is a man's best friend.
—AUSTIN PHELPS

◆   ◆   ◆

Writing a check when we do not have the money in our account is illegal. Bouncing a check is breaking the law. Because most of us don't get sent to jail but instead get slapped with overdraft fees, we don't take it too seriously. We're only disappointed with ourselves for having incurred more debt and for having nothing to show for it.

If we've been negligent with our checking account—if we've been intuiting how much money we have in it rather than balancing the numbers—it's time to start over. We can start fresh by opening a new account. Or, we can stop using our account for a month or two and use money orders to pay our bills.

Today, one way or another, I will work toward a balanced checking account.

◆   ◆   ◆

August 16

The human species, according to the best theory
I can form of it, is composed of two distinct races:
the men who borrow and the men who lend.

—CHARLES LAMB

❖ ❖ ❖

Debt separates us; it puts us into categories. We are borrowers, or we are lenders. The borrowers get behind while the lenders get ahead—financially, at least.

Our creditors are not "bad" because they're getting ahead while we're going under. Our neighbor is not "bad" because she earns a two-comma income. Everyone makes choices, for better or for worse. We don't need to belittle others for making different choices. We focus on living with our choices, on learning from them, and on striving to make the best choices now and in the future.

Today I will accept that it's okay for others to be wealthy, even at my expense.

❖ ❖ ❖

August 17

Beautiful credit! The foundation of modern society.
Who shall say that this is not the golden age of mutual
trust, of unlimited reliance upon human promises?
This peculiar condition of society . . . puts into the
mouth of a distinguished speculator in lands and mines
this remark: "I wasn't worth a cent two years ago,
and now I owe two millions of dollars."

—MARK TWAIN

◆ ◆ ◆

Most of us see credit as a natural part of life. We
were born into a society that accepts credit as a
means to an end—even expects it.

If we think it through, credit is a "peculiar condition
of society." One minute we don't have a dime to spend.
As soon as we get a credit card in the mail, we consider
ourselves five thousand dollars "richer." We charge our
five thousand dollars and instantly we transform from
a state of having to a state of owing. The concept is simple yet peculiar.

Today I will consider how
I view the concept of credit.

◆ ◆ ◆

August 18

Our lives improve only when we take chances—
and the first and most difficult risk we can take
is to be honest with ourselves.

—WALTER ANDERSON

♦ ♦ ♦

In the United States, gambling has gone mainstream.
State governments run lotteries, casinos cater to children, pull tabs are sold in bars, and a casino can be found no more than a two-hour drive away from most households.

Gambling is not a new concept in the United States, and in all likelihood it won't ever go away, so we need to be aware that gambling is not all fun and games. For an estimated 3 to 5 percent of the U.S. population, gambling is a chronic illness—an addiction they cannot control. For those individuals and their families, gambling causes financial devastation, job loss, crime, and broken homes.

**Today, before I introduce a loved one to gambling,
I will consider the potential damage.**

♦ ♦ ♦

August 19

Dignity is a veil between us and the real truth.
—EDWIN P. WHIPPLE

❖ ❖ ❖

To some of us, credit cards give us our dignity. We feel important, mature, respected, and financially capable when we present our plastic to the clerk. We panic at the thought of cutting up our cards or closing our accounts. Without our cards, we'd feel empty, alone, and inadequate.

Credit cards are our cover. We use them as a shield against the emptiness, loneliness, and inadequacy we feel inside. We ask ourselves whether we want to go through life hiding behind a shield or whether we want to be bold and expose our true selves—perceived weaknesses and all. When we open ourselves up to the pain, we give ourselves an opportunity to get through it. We also give ourselves a chance to see who and what we really are.

Today I will know that I am most lovable when I am myself—weaknesses, vulnerabilities, and all.

❖ ❖ ❖

August 20

The art of being wise is the art
of knowing what to overlook.

—WILLIAM JAMES

◆　　◆　　◆

We may have made some changes in our lifestyle. Instead of going out to eat three times a week, we go out once a week. We refuse invitations to go to the mall because it's a slippery place.

When we change, the people who know us well are going to react. They may be pleased, perplexed, inspired, mad, cynical, hurt, annoyed, or devastated. While we need to remain sensitive to how we relay the information, we cannot let the reactions of others—or our thoughts about how people will react—deter us from making a move we know in our heart is right for us. We are not defined by the reactions of others.

Today I will be bold.

◆　　◆　　◆

August 21

We learn to be spontaneous and free as we grow
in self-awareness and self-esteem. Spontaneity
emerges as our confidence and trust in ourselves
increase, and we become more secure in our ability
to maintain healthy boundaries.

—MELODY BEATTIE

◆　◆　◆

Depending on what our issues are, we may have gotten to a point where we don't allow ourselves to
have any fun. We may not even know *how* to have fun
anymore. We say we can't spend the money. It would
be selfish. What we're saying is that we're not
worthy of a good time. We've been *bad*. We feel
ashamed. Laughing and having a good time would
make us feel like we're putting up a front. We're not
happy with ourselves. Why should we act like we're
enjoying life?

Having fun is a basic need. We all *need* fun and laughter. We don't always need to spend a lot of money to
have fun—and sometimes we do need to spend some.
But fun can be simple. The first step is telling ourselves
that we deserve to have fun and that we are worthy.
We get past the shame of our debt or addiction by talking to others. As we open up to others, we open up to
fun.

Today I will do something spontaneous.

◆　◆　◆

August 22

If you do not find peace in yourself,
you will never find it anywhere else.
—PAULA A. BENDRY

❖　❖　❖

We long for someone or something, believing it will make us complete. If we marry rich, we won't have to worry. If we have money, we'll be complete. Deep down, we know we're misguided because we're reacting to our external circumstances.

We can hope and wish and pray for our life to improve yet get no results—or get into even more trying circumstances. The power of making good things happen lies in praying with our heart, knowing we're complete whether we get what we want or not, and ending our prayer with "Thy will be done." In doing so, we know we stay on our path.

Today I will know that when life feels as if it isn't moving forward, I'm probably the one responsible for blocking its progress.

❖　❖　❖

August 23

No one can make you feel inferior without your consent.
—ELEANOR ROOSEVELT

◆　◆　◆

We already carry more shame than we can handle. When collection agencies start calling, badgering, threatening lawsuits, and verbally abusing us to try to get money, we feel bad, little, and worthless. They catch us off guard. We're in the middle of dinner, we have friends over, or we just sat down for some needed peace and quiet or to play with our children. Sometimes we get mad—especially if we didn't create the debt but must put up with the calls.

We don't have to tolerate abuse from anybody. Abusive behavior is not acceptable. If we're feeling particularly vulnerable when a collector calls, we firmly tell him or her that we will need to communicate in writing from now on. Or we make arrangements to call back at a specified date and time. If the agent continues to hound us, we hang up and turn off the answering machine. We know our intentions are good, and we will discuss them in a healthy atmosphere with someone we consider to be a business associate.

Today I will know that nobody gets to abuse me in any way.

◆　◆　◆

August 24

To do good and to communicate forget not:
for with such sacrifices God is well pleased.

—HEBREWS 11:1

◆　◆　◆

We know we need to call our creditors, to set things straight, and to tell them we're in over our heads, but we don't want to do it. We feel inferior, inadequate, and foolish. We're intimidated. We fear their response.

We just need to prepare for the call. We talk to our support group. We may even want to write a script so we'll remember everything we need to say. We usually find that our creditors respond favorably to our honesty. Even loan sharks would much rather know they can get something rather than nothing. Afterward, we feel an incredible sense of relief. We also gain confidence. We did what we said we were going to do—and it worked.

**Today I will trust that when I do the
right thing I will get the best result.**

◆　◆　◆

August 25

Where talent is a dwarf, self-esteem is a giant.

—J. PETIT-SENN

◆　◆　◆

Creditors are used to negotiating with clients who cannot make minimum payments. They negotiate interest rates, monthly payments, and may even forgive part of the total balance due. When we call, they are prepared. They know what to say. We are not unique to them. They've heard it all before. They won't be surprised. They were hired to deal with people like us. It's their job.

Because some people are very good at their jobs, we need to be prepared. Some of us, however, may not feel that negotiation is our strength. We make up for it by being ready emotionally to make the call. We need to feel determined and articulate. If we run across an employee who tries to harass us, who tries to convince us to change our terms, we employ what's called "the broken record." We repeat, calmly and firmly, our stance, regardless of what the creditor says.

Today I will stand by the financial commitment I've determined I can make to any given creditor.

◆　◆　◆

August 26

I'm so happy to be rich, I'm willing
to take all the consequences.
—HOWARD ABRAHAMSON

◆　◆　◆

Having an addiction or poor spending patterns and having access to a well that doesn't run dry is a challenge. The consequences that we feel are more internal than external. We feel bad and unhappy. But we still have a nice house, car, and money to blow. We think we're only hurting ourselves, so why change? What's our motivation?

We humbly acknowledge that regardless of how much money we have, we're still human. We still have spirits that need to soar. Our core motivations are the same as everyone else's—peace of mind and happiness. To get there, we take the same basic course as everyone else. We become true to ourselves, others, and our Higher Power. We take responsibility.

Today I will know that change starts with humility.

◆　◆　◆

August 27

To understand everything makes one tolerant.

—MADAME DE STAËL

❖　❖　❖

Many of us get down on ourselves for spending more money than we have, for not making enough money, for not taking care of ourselves, for being a "bad" parent, and for making poor choices. The worse we feel about ourselves, the deeper we fall. Instead of improving our behavior, we do something self-destructive—something to reflect how we feel about ourselves.

When we find that we're feeling intolerant of ourselves and others, we discipline ourselves by countering every self-destructive thought with a positive action. Instead of having a drink to calm our nerves, we have a soothing cup of tea. Instead of going shopping to help change our mood, we pray and meditate. We also accept that we are human and that making mistakes and feeling inadequate are part of being human. Lastly, we remind ourselves of all the things we do well and right. As we manage to tolerate ourselves, we also learn to tolerate others.

Today I will remember that my intentions are pure.

❖　❖　❖

August 28

Forget regret, or life is yours to miss.

—JONATHON LARSON

◆　◆　◆

Our thoughts drift to our regrets. We wonder how our life would be today if we'd done things differently. If we'd taken some risks or made better choices, maybe we'd be happier. Maybe those around us would be happier. By making the wrong choices, did we throw off our Higher Power's plan for us? What ripple effect have our actions had? Every day we blame ourselves for screwing up.

Life gets better if we clear our heads of the past and concentrate on the choices we make now, in the present. Regardless of what we've done, we can still make a difference. But we need to be here, now, in the present. in touch with ourselves, others, and our Higher Power. We always need to be moving forward. Always.

**Today I will focus on making wise choices—
big and small—now, in the present, that
will work to create a promising future.**

◆　◆　◆

August 29

Nothing is more terrible than ignorance in action.
—JOHANN WOLFGANG VON GOETHE

◆　◆　◆

We may have a very clear understanding of how we got into debt. We may know exactly who, what, when, where, and why as well. We may have even expected our plight. Those of us who really don't know how we got into debt benefit from reviewing our debting history. When did it start—what was our first debt? What was our thinking? Our attitude? What did we do or not do to keep us in debt? When did we start feeling bad and hopeless about our debt?

Knowing our history helps us to make wiser choices now. We replace ignorance with awareness. Instead of blindly taking steps that get us deeper into debt, we base our actions on what we know to be true about ourselves and our circumstances.

Today I will take time to get to know myself better by reviewing my debting history.

◆　◆　◆

August 30

[Jealousy is] a kind of civil war in the soul.

—WILLIAM PENN

◆ ◆ ◆

The ugly green-eyed monster pops up every now and then. Some of us see it quite often. We want the beautiful car and house that our friend owns either because we've never had them or because we've lost them. We hear someone at work who's always wearing new clothes talk about their exotic vacation. The desire to have these things is fine in and of itself. But when we make enemies of others for having what we admire or want, we become emotionally, mentally, and spiritually unhealthy.

We instead replace the negative emotion of jealousy with positive thoughts. We thank others for having what we want because they are setting an example for us, reminding us that all is achievable. We compliment them and tell them we admire what they have. In doing so, we create positive, wondrous feelings for ourselves (and others).

Today I will compliment someone.

◆ ◆ ◆

August 31

A man without ambition is dead. A man with ambition
but no love is dead. A man with ambition and love for
his blessings here on earth is ever so alive.

—PEARL BAILEY

❖ ❖ ❖

Is our glass half full or half empty? We may see ourselves as positive people, but when we take the time
to examine our thoughts closely, we may be surprised.
We may have a lot to complain about, but so what? We
can choose misery or happiness. It's all in how we see
that glass.

Instead of griping about bills, we become thankful for
the money that is coming in. Instead of thinking about
what activities we're missing in our lives, we're grateful for the solitude. Instead of being hurt by what
friends and family aren't doing, we feel blessed we have
them in our lives in the first place.

**Today I will humble myself by counting my blessings,
knowing that without them I would truly be lost.**

❖ ❖ ❖

September 1

Realism is to think that two and two
is four and neither five nor three.

—A. E. HOUSMAN

◆　◆　◆

If someone asked us today, this moment, how much money we had and how much debt we had, many of us would have a hard time answering. Most of us have money in more than one place. We'd have to dig out the paperwork on stocks and bonds, pension plans, IRAs, savings and checking accounts. We'd have to total balances due.

We make it a point to know exactly how much money we have at any given moment. We call the twenty-four-hour banking service to get an accurate daily balance. If necessary, we use a computer program to balance our checkbook. We tally our payments after paying credit cards and loans so we know our remaining balances due. We diligently track the paper trail. In doing so, we gain knowledge, which gives us a base from which to make intelligent decisions.

Today I will do some math.

◆　◆　◆

September 2

Creativity can solve almost any problem.
The creative act, the defeat of habit
by originality, overcomes everything.

—GEORGE LOIS

◆ ◆ ◆

We come home from work, empty the mailbox, and toss the bills on the table. Receipts and unpaid bills are left in piles. We don't know what exactly needs our attention. We despise the thought of dealing with the mess. Why should we give our debt any more energy than we already give it?

It's easy to have respect for people, nature, and art. What's probably last on our mind is respecting what gives us grief—our debt. Debt (or compound interest!) is a powerful force. We learn to work with it, not against it. We thank our debt by creating a ritual for paying it. We devise a special place, a basket or box, where we carefully place bills as they come in. We give order to the mess. We gain momentum through our debt's power.

**Today I will work with the power of my debt
by creating rituals for the act of paying my bills.**

◆ ◆ ◆

September 3

Truth is the knowledge of what is just
and what is lawful.

—EPICTETUS

◆ ◆ ◆

Bankruptcy used to be a dirty word, but people are now declaring bankruptcy in record numbers, and the stigma is disappearing.

When it comes to declaring bankruptcy, there is no right or wrong. Bankruptcy laws exist for a reason. While it's fairly easy to declare bankruptcy, and while some of us (especially those of us who are dealing with chronic illness or who've experienced serious unexpected business losses) have no choice, the rest of us need to remember the laws by which we live.

If we're compulsive spenders or gamblers, declaring bankruptcy won't solve our problems. We'll be back in court in another five years or so unless we address the real emotional and spiritual issues complicating our behavior. If we're the spouse of an addict, we need to remember the choices we've made.

Today I will ask myself why another person or a company should be responsible for absorbing my debt.

◆ ◆ ◆

September 4

The surest way to ruin a man who doesn't know
how to handle money is to give him some.

—GEORGE BERNARD SHAW

◆　◆　◆

The bottom line for many of us is that we need to
become good stewards of our money, which takes
skill and practice. The fact that we've never learned the
skills or put them into practice does not make us less
of a person. It simply means that, for whatever reason,
we've chosen to focus our attention elsewhere.

Learning to manage our money is within reach. The
skills we can acquire; the discipline we can force until
it becomes second nature.

**Today I will call a consumer credit
counseling service and sign up for
a free money management course.**

◆　◆　◆

September 5

Information is of two kinds. We know
a subject ourselves, or we know where
we can find information upon it.
—SAMUEL JOHNSON

◆ ◆ ◆

Knowledge is power. The more information we have, the more empowered we feel. The unknown can be scary. We don't know what we're getting into so we don't act at all. When we know our legal rights and obligations, we start making decisions we feel good about. We can confront difficult situations with confidence instead of fear.

We can get information about our legal rights concerning debt and divorce or debt and collection agencies by visiting the library, a lawyer, Debtors Anonymous meetings, financial advisers, and nonprofit consumer credit agencies.

Today I will make it my responsibility to learn as much as I can about my debt and related legal issues.

◆ ◆ ◆

September 6

Wisdom is knowing what to do next.
—HERBERT HOOVER

♦ ♦ ♦

We've all heard stories of people who've been denied credit because of faulty credit reports. The potential for error is great, especially if we've gone through divorce.

Just as we want to be informed about how much money our IRA is making or how much interest a credit card charges, we want to know what the various credit agencies have on our file. Three agencies currently disperse credit reports. We're wise to contact each one to be assured that the files are up to date.

Today I will arrange to get copies of my credit reports.

♦ ♦ ♦

September 7

I'd like to live as a poor man with lots of money.
—PABLO PICASSO

◆ ◆ ◆

Some of us were taught not to place a lot of value on money. After all, it's only money, and money can't buy happiness. True enough. While many of us don't place much value on money, we manage to value the possessions that money can buy. The result is that we treat money frivolously and spend it recklessly.

We know it's true that love and the quality of our relationships are far more valuable than money. We also know we can't put a price tag on good health. We begin, however, to appreciate and to value money for what it is—a means to an end and a responsibility. When we value money, we're less likely to spend it carelessly or frivolously. We're more likely to save it and to put it to good use.

Today I give my cash the same value I place on my most treasured material possessions.

◆ ◆ ◆

September 8

> There is only one success—to be able
> to spend your life in your own way.
>
> —CHRISTOPHER MORLEY

◆　◆　◆

Some of us find comfort in debt. It gives us a reason to go to work; paying it gives us something to work toward. We're so used to having debt, we wouldn't know what to do or how to act if we had money to throw around. We're afraid of what we might become. Would others despise or resent us? Would we become ultracontrolling, afraid that others only want to take advantage of us? Would we deny ourselves and others for fear of being too ostentatious?

Having money creates a whole new set of challenges. We remember that we are defined neither by our savings accounts nor by what appearances we keep up. To be out of debt—to be moving toward financial abundance—gives us opportunities. We make a conscious effort to uphold our values and to maintain supportive friendships. We don't sabotage the opportunity to become wealthy by mistrusting it.

**Today I will trust myself to fully
meet the challenges of being wealthy.**

◆　◆　◆

September 9

The only thing I can't stand is discomfort.
—GLORIA STEINEM

✦ ✦ ✦

With no cash (or credit cards) in our pockets, we may end up saying "no" to a lot in life. No, we can't go to a movie, take a vacation, buy that dress, or get a massage. We can't afford it. We'd feel guilty for spending what we don't have. But in the end, we feel deprived. Our needs to socialize, to take a break, and to take care of ourselves are not being met.

Feelings of deprivation can lead us to impulsive or compulsive spending. We may not typically spend a hundred dollars every time we go to a Target, Wal-Mart, or Kmart. We may not typically splurge on a two-thousand-dollar tractor lawn mower. But when we feel deprived, we feel a strong need to compensate by treating ourselves.

Today I will accept that it's okay and necessary to spend money meeting the physical, emotional, mental, and spiritual needs that I've identified on my spending plan.

✦ ✦ ✦

September 10

The best and safest thing is to keep a balance
in your life, acknowledge the great powers around us
and in us. If you can do that, and live that way,
you are really a wise man.

—EURIPIDES

◆ ◆ ◆

We have a deadline, a goal, or a second job. We develop a mind-set that the project is all we can focus on. We obsess and worry about getting it done and put much of our life on hold. We miss workouts, family gatherings, baseball games, and dinner with friends. Meanwhile, we don't accomplish as much as we'd planned to get done. We get frustrated. We feel deprived.

We stop and remember that life does not revolve around one situation or one deadline—at least not for long. We acknowledge that getting out of debt or making more money is a piece of our life, but it is not the center of our life. When a situation becomes all-consuming, we remember the other parts of our life. We continue to engage in the rest of life while we pay our debt.

**Today I will turn my trying situation over to
my Higher Power and enjoy a positive situation
in my life.**

◆ ◆ ◆

September 11

Nothing contributes so much to tranquilizing the mind
as a steady purpose—a point on which the soul may
fire its intellectual eye.

—MARY WOLLSTONECRAFT SHELLEY

◆　◆　◆

More Americans are getting rich now than ever
before. And those who are doing it are doing it
quickly. Stock options (offered by corporations to
employees), day-trading (trading stocks on-line), and
Internet-based companies can reap millions, sometimes
without the long, grueling hours and hard work we associate with achieving the American Dream. Not being
part of this whirlwind can make us feel like we're all
dressed up with no place to go. We want to be part of
the action, but we don't have a plan. We begin to feel
desperate and restless.

This type of energy is strong and easily sucks in those
of us who do not have a clear sense of direction. Rather
than get tossed about in the eye of the storm, we stop
and take time to get centered. We reach for the game
plan that feels right to us—not for whatever is popular
at the time.

Today I will own my true destiny.

◆　◆　◆

September 12

I cannot accept my feelings selectively; even despair
I must acknowledge despite my fear of its darkness.

—UNKNOWN

◆ ◆ ◆

We may get desperate after a big loss in a casino,
after our spouse divorces us for another, or
when a loved one is dying.

Desperation is emotion and energy without a plan.
The strength of the emotion and energy can take us far,
but it can take us in the wrong direction fast. We want
to take action, but we're frustrated and confused.

Desperation is a sign that we need to sort through
our thoughts and feelings. Before we take any action,
we write about our thoughts and feelings of injustice
and hopelessness in a journal or talk to a supportive
friend.

**Today I will not act out of desperation;
I will center myself before taking any action
I might later regret.**

◆ ◆ ◆

September 13

Our job is not to straighten each other out,
but to help each other up.
—NEVA COLE

◆　◆　◆

When we get into trouble with money and are ready to seek help, our first thought may be to talk to a financial planner or someone else who understands money management. While this is a promising first step, the help our financial planner gives us will probably end with the spending plan he or she has prepared for us.

Our support system needs to be twofold. We need money management skills, but our greatest support comes from people who will help us stay on our spending plan and change destructive behaviors. This may involve dealing with a host of emotions related to compulsive spending, gambling, codependency—the list can go on and on.

Today I will talk to someone who can help me.

◆　◆　◆

September 14

The best thing we do in life is when we do good
to others and get nothing in return—for the good
will be waiting for us in the end.

—MAMA D.

◆　◆　◆

Right now, we may need to lean on others. We may
need to release troubling thoughts and emotions
about the cause of our money problems. We may need
to rely on the energy of others until we're strong
enough to create our own inertia. At that point, we may
find ourselves helping others with the same problems
we struggled with not too long ago.

When others come to us looking for help, we take
the time and energy to help them. We've been there,
we know how it feels, and we can be compassionate.
Only by helping others are we able to keep the serenity we've found.

**Today I will know that my serenity
depends on "giving it back."**

◆　◆　◆

September 15

> To go with the drift of things,
> To yield with a grace to reason,
> And to bow and accept the end
> of a love or a season.
>
> —ROBERT FROST

◆　◆　◆

We can beat ourselves up for losing or spending too much, or we can accept who we are and what we've done and start taking responsibility. We're not bad because we overspend, gamble, drink or drug in excess, spend compulsively, are chronically ill, or live with someone who does or is any of the above. We don't like ourselves for doing or being whatever it is that increases our unsecured debt. We accept that, with support, we can change what we don't like, whether it's our attitude or our behavior. But if we dwell on what we don't like, it only lingers.

We know that a consequence of our addiction or our lack of awareness is a seemingly uncontrollable amount of unsecured debt. By recognizing and accepting that our behavior has caused our debt, we can move on to the next season.

**Today I will stop beating myself up
and get to the heart of the problem.**

◆　◆　◆

September 16

> He that considers how little he dwells upon
> the condition of others will learn how little
> attention of others is attracted by himself.
>
> —SAMUEL JOHNSON

◆　　◆　　◆

When we're mad at ourselves, we tend to take it out on everyone else. We're irritable, we don't smile, we yell at family members, and self-defeating thoughts run through our heads. The crabbier we get, the worse we feel.

It's okay to be irritable now and then, but we learn how to snap out of it. We know that love heals and moves all. To generate love for others, we must first love ourselves—with all our faults. We ask ourselves what's truly bothering us. What's making us feel so bad? Are we fed up with our body for failing us? Do we feel we gamble, spend, or drink too much? Do we feel unlovable? Are we treating others or ourselves poorly? Are others treating us poorly?

We keep the heart of the matter in mind, while we admit to ourselves that we're feeling irritable. We accept the feeling. We tell ourselves we love ourselves when we feel this way. As the feeling of love starts to envelop us, we start to heal. We feel better and see things differently.

**Today I will identify my feelings
and thank myself for feeling them.**

◆　　◆　　◆

September 17

No one can avoid aging, but aging
productively is something else.
—KATHERINE GRAHAM

◆　◆　◆

We're getting married and so in love we can't even
think about divorce or any potential money
problems that could arise. We're young and haven't
even gotten our first "real" job yet. Why would we start
thinking about saving for retirement?

The way we see money when we're nineteen years
old is not necessarily how we'll see it at age sixty. The
more experiences we have with money and spending
patterns, the more likely we are to change our thinking about money. How we prepare for the future is
based on our current thoughts and attitudes. So it's
important, for financial planning purposes, to take a big
leap in time. If we accept that after the next twenty-four
hours we'll be different—if only on a molecular level—
than we are right now, we can only imagine how different we'll be in the years to come.

Today I accept that I will change.

◆　◆　◆

September 18

A man who has committed a mistake and
doesn't correct it is committing another mistake.

—Confucius

◆ ◆ ◆

Taking personal inventory means looking at ourselves with rigorous honesty and making two lists—one of our good points and another of our bad points. What behaviors serve us and others well, and what behaviors cause trouble or grief?

We may have a vague sense, in the back of our minds, of what we'd like to change about ourselves. Thinking it through, putting it on paper, puts it in the forefront. We see clearly how we can improve our lives. If we work on changing the negative behaviors, our lives begin to improve automatically. At the end of each day, we review our behavior for the day—take an inventory of ourselves. We pray and ask our Higher Power for forgiveness; we apologize in our prayers or openly the next day to anyone we've harmed. We correct our mistakes; we move forward.

**Today, before falling asleep, I will
review my behavior for the day.**

◆ ◆ ◆

September 19

It is far easier to act under conditions
of tyranny than to think.

—HANNAH ARENDT

❖ ❖ ❖

Some people have caused some serious consequences in our lives. Our addicted spouse got us fifty thousand dollars in debt, a drunken driver put us in a wheelchair for life, our former spouse left us with three children and no support, or our boss underpays us. We ask ourselves why these troublesome people have had such a powerful impact on our lives.

We don't need to make excuses for people who've caused us trouble, but we can't go on blaming them forever. It all comes back to choices. At some point, we made a choice to marry our spouse, to go down the same road the drunken driver happened to be on, to have children, or to work for a particular employer. True, we could not have known the consequences beforehand. We trust that to encounter these particular people at a particular time is our Higher Power's way of giving us yet another life lesson.

Today I will ask myself what I have
learned from my toughest teachers—
those who've caused hardship in my life.

❖ ❖ ❖

September 20

A penny saved is a penny earned.
—BENJAMIN FRANKLIN

◆　◆　◆

The little piece of copper we call a penny doesn't seem to garner the respect it once did. For one, it doesn't buy what it used to. Also, those of us too lazy to give the exact amount when paying for something end up weighing down our purses and pant pockets; we collect but don't spend them. Restaurants and shops keep small trays of extra pennies on countertops for patrons to take from or to contribute to. No one seems to worry that the tray will be stolen.

Pennies—just like nickels, dimes, and quarters—add up. Pennies are also just as capable of compounding interest as any other form of money. We give the penny its due respect. We keep a jar or other container in which we place our pennies and other spare change. Once it's full, we may find we have enough change to make a credit card payment or to buy an airline ticket.

Today I will find a container in which to store extra change, and I will keep it in a convenient place.

◆　◆　◆

September 21

Some people regard discipline as a chore. For me,
it is a kind of order that sets me free to fly.

—JULIE ANDREWS

◆　◆　◆

We've finally managed to pay off the car or a credit card debt; our youngest just started school and we'll no longer be paying as much for day care. When the bills disappear, what happens to the money? For many of us, it seems to disappear as well.

We make plans for our money. When we pay off one credit card, we take the monthly payment and apply it to another card. When we finally own our car (and don't have any credit card debt), we put that monthly sum into a savings account and use it for a down payment on our next car. When the kids are out of day care, we use that money to save for their college.

Closing one account is a good time to revisit our spending plan. Maybe we divert one or two payments toward a vacation or take a portion of the payment and add it to a basic need category. We can celebrate our accomplishment, but we remember the importance of having a plan for our money.

Today I will review my spending plan.

◆　◆　◆

September 22

Love is not . . . a noun. It is a verb.

—HUGH DOWNS

◆　◆　◆

We all have responsibilities, such as paying bills, that we want to avoid. The more we dread something, the more awful we make it. We put more energy into avoiding it than we do into actually doing it.

We change our frame of mind. It may seem silly at first, but we tell ourselves we love doing it. We say it out loud. In doing so, we propel ourselves into action. We get the job done faster and with less energy than we'd imagined. Over time, we may actually grow to love the job.

Today I will love doing everything I do.

◆　◆　◆

September 23

Realism is the art of depicting nature
as it is seen by toads.

—AMBROSE BIERCE

◆　◆　◆

We find an ad in the paper for the perfect job. We're confident we'll be given a promotion. We're so sure, we put all our attention on what we feel entitled to and neglect other possibilities. Every decision we make is based on what we want to happen. We buy a new suit not because we want to but because we feel it's important to impress our boss. We don't bother sending out other résumés, because we know the job we interviewed for yesterday is ours. We put all our eggs in one basket. If the basket drops, so does our morale. Where do we go from here? We feel disappointed and resentful because we didn't get what we felt entitled to.

We remember the choice we made to put all of our eggs in one basket. We stop obsessing about a certain outcome. We live our lives as if the possibilities are endless. We make choices based on what feels right for us, not on what will achieve a certain outcome. We stop manipulating circumstances. We learn that what is ours will come to us if we let it.

**Today, when making decisions, I will stop
and think about what feels right to me.**

◆　◆　◆

September 24

A friend is one who knows you
and loves you just the same.

—ELBERT HUBBARD

◆　◆　◆

Our best friend is having a kitchen utensil party or a candle party—some kind of home shopping get-together. We feel obligated to attend. We may have plastic bowls falling out of our cupboards and enough candles to light up the town, but she's our best friend. We need to support her.

We do need to support our friends, but above all we need to take care of ourselves. We step away from our devotion and get objective. The makers of these products know that they'll make extra sales in the name of friendships. Why should we fall prey to this marketing strategy?

We know we have a compulsive spending or debting problem. We know home shopping is a slippery place. Plastic bowls are not on our spending plan. We kindly decline. If the host is our best friend, she'll understand that by attending her party we'd be jeopardizing our solvency. If she's not our best friend, we don't need to explain our debting problem. We kindly, but firmly and confidently, decline.

**Today I will not jeopardize my solvency
by worrying about how others might
react to my new, healthy behaviors.**

◆　◆　◆

September 25

Patience means waiting without anxiety.

—SAINT FRANCIS DE SALES

◆　◆　◆

Most of us did not get into debt overnight. It took a long time. At first we felt good and in control. Later we had only a vague awareness of what we were doing with our money and credit cards. Eventually, our debt spiraled out of control, making our lives unmanageable.

Getting out of debt takes some time, too. We've committed to paying all our debts, usually only a fraction at a time. At the end of the year, we may look at the amount of debt liquidated versus the amount due and feel despair.

We remember that because we are changing our behaviors or have in one way or another separated from a gambler or debtor, we are well ahead. Had we not committed to a spending plan and to paying our creditors honestly and with integrity, we'd be deeper in debt.

**Today I will credit myself for the progress
I've made in all areas of my life.**

◆　◆　◆

September 26

Credit is a device that gets better the less it is used.
—ANONYMOUS

◆　◆　◆

If we're applying for a mortgage or a loan, the lending organization gets a copy of our credit report. One factor in determining whether we're a safe bet is the amount of open credit we have. Open credit is the unspent amount on our credit cards. If we, for instance, have a $7,000 limit on one credit card, and we have $2,200 of available credit, the lending organization will not see our debt as being $4,800. They will see it for what it has the potential to be—$7,000.

To eliminate open credit, we need to close credit card accounts we're still paying off. Most companies do so upon request, although some will try to talk us out of it. Closing an account, however, is our choice. It's a simple phone call or letter.

Today I will close unnecessary accounts.

◆　◆　◆

September 27

In God we trust; all others must pay cash.

—AMERICAN PROVERB

◆ ◆ ◆

We all know that cash is money. Cash is the crisp dollar bills, the shiny coins, and even to a certain extent the decorative checks we write. Cash is real. Cash is the truth. Cash is, for the most part, finite. What we have is what we have.

When we start using symbols for cash, we suddenly lose our senses. We can't afford to buy the coat with cash, but we can afford it with a credit card. We can't leave the blackjack table when we have stacks of chips to play with, but if the chips were twenty-dollar bills, we'd wonder what we were doing playing with our money.

Today I will remember that cash equals reality.

◆ ◆ ◆

September 28

"He means well" is useless unless he does well.

—PLAUTUS

◆　◆　◆

When debt overwhelms us, we feel hopeless. We want to pay it all off or avoid it entirely. If we do deal with creditors, we agree to pay more than we can. In our heads, it's all or nothing. We see no middle ground.

We create payment schedules that we and our creditors can work with—schedules that hurt neither us nor our creditors. We need to have enough money to meet basic needs so we don't go deeper in debt. Our creditors need to know we have the best intention to meet our obligations. If necessary, we get help through a nonprofit credit counseling service.

Today I will listen to reason. I will have the best intentions to pay my debt while taking care of myself and my family.

◆　◆　◆

September 29

Life is not a problem to be solved
but a reality to be experienced.

—SØREN KIERKEGAARD

◆ ◆ ◆

Our debt is spiraling so out of control we can't face it. We can't tolerate sitting at the table one more time trying to manipulate figures to meet the month's expenses. If we're responsible for creating the debt, we may be in denial or have a lot of shame. If our spouse is responsible, we may be so confused we give up, not knowing whether he or she will come home from the casino with a fistful of cash or another grand or two in the hole. We're tired of creating solutions to get through the debt. We give up. We bury our heads in the sand like an ostrich. If we pull our heads up, we're afraid we'll have a nervous breakdown.

The ostrich stage is a normal human reaction to overwhelming circumstances. We can only take so much. But in the ostrich stage, we make ourselves especially vulnerable. We may return responsibility for paying bills to our gambling spouse. We may agree to sign credit card applications in our name. We may accumulate hundreds of dollars worth of overdraft fees.

If we've reached the ostrich stage, we seek outside support from someone we can trust to handle our finances—to shed light on what we cannot seem to see.

**Today instead of staying in the
ostrich stage, I will seek help.**

◆ ◆ ◆

September 30

When all is said and done, willingness is everything.

—FRANK D.

◆　◆　◆

We have a simple goal, such as to start writing down our expenses daily. Some of us, however, have a hard time getting started. The task seems simple enough, so why don't we just do it?

We stop stumbling over the missing details, and we think it through. What is it that we need to get started? Is it that we can't decide what to record our expenses on or what the best method is? We identify the small steps—in this case finding the right tool and method—toward reaching our goal. We try to think of solutions. How do other people do this? Maybe someone else can suggest a means. We allow ourselves to proceed, perhaps without using the best method. We buy a small notebook or use a calendar.

Today I will just do it.

◆　◆　◆

October 1

My philosophy is that not only are you responsible
for your life, but doing the best at this moment
puts you in the best place for the next moment.

—OPRAH WINFREY

❖   ❖   ❖

When we've got ten different credit card bills, four
loans, plus living expenses, it can all pile up—literally. We fumble through stacks of papers that need
to be sorted and filed. We bury a bill and are charged
a late fee, the result of not uncovering it in time. All
the clutter contributes to the chaos we feel inside.

The external is a reflection of the internal; how we
keep our surroundings is related to how we feel inside.
We get organized. We throw away unnecessary papers,
and we make files for what we need to keep. If we have
a computer, we consider using inexpensive money
management software to keep track of our finances. As
the external world clears, the internal world is soothed.

**Today I will sort through paperwork, knowing
that order increases my level of serenity.**

❖   ❖   ❖

October 2

God heals, and the doctor takes the fees.
—BENJAMIN FRANKLIN

◆ ◆ ◆

When we need cash, many of us rely on automatic teller machines. They're located conveniently at gas stations, grocery stores, and casinos. ATMs located at places of convenience, however, usually charge a fee—anywhere from one to three dollars—for service. We may stop at the ATM three or four times over a two-week period. Four or eight dollars may not seem like a lot, but it adds up quickly, and when we're only withdrawing twenty or thirty dollars at a time, that's about 5 percent of our take!

Convenience costs money, and that's okay sometimes. We, however, plan to visit only those ATMs that charge no fees. We refuse to use ATMs that charge fees unless absolutely necessary. We become aware.

Today I will call my bank and find out where I can use my ATM card without paying a fee.

◆ ◆ ◆

October 3

Change is the only thing that has brought progress.
—CHARLES F. KETTERING

❖　❖　❖

For those of us trying to abolish credit card debt and use, destroying our cards is a logical step. But what about transactions that seem to require a credit card, such as reserving a hotel room, buying an airplane ticket, renting a car, or ordering flowers? Credit cards are standard fare these days. The business world expects patrons to have them.

If we truly want to erase credit card debt and live with cash, we consider the debit card. Debit cards go against a checking or savings account, so we're not actually borrowing money—we're using our own money just as if we were writing a check. Most banks offer them and may charge a small fee for this service. We consider whether paying the fee for a debit card will in the long run save us money by keeping credit cards out of our life.

Today I will not debt.

❖　❖　❖

October 4

What's money? A man is a success in life if he
gets up in the morning and goes to bed at night
and in between does what he wants to do.

—BOB DYLAN

◆　◆　◆

Those of us who choose to live a simple life, who
aren't driven to successful careers, big homes, or
nights on the town, are seen by some on the surface as
being boring, dull, or unmotivated. Action-seekers can't
seem to relate. We sense we're being judged for our
lifestyle choices. We feel others perceive us as under-
achievers, people who are unwilling or unable to take
risks.

We imagine ourselves with a different lifestyle. How
comfortable or uncomfortable do we feel? We remember that living a simple life is a choice based on values
and goals. We remember our values and goals.

Today I will trust in my own choices.

◆　◆　◆

October 5

Time is money. . . . And very good money
to those who reckon interest by it.
—CHARLES DICKENS

◆ ◆ ◆

Time is money, and money takes time. Between paying bills, calling bankers and credit card companies, organizing paperwork, recording and calculating expenses, writing and revising spending plans, balancing checkbooks, visiting banks and ATMs, cutting coupons, and searching for the best deals, we may need to devote an average of a few hours a week to managing our money.

Although the time spent organizing our money varies for each of us, we need to commit to taking the time. In doing so, we establish that money management is a priority in our life.

**Today I will accept that money management,
like eating, is a necessity.**

◆ ◆ ◆

October 6

Progress is the activity of today
and the assurance of tomorrow.
—RALPH WALDO EMERSON

◆　◆　◆

We may be at a point where no one wants our business. They'll give us some credit, all right, but it's a very low credit limit and a very high interest rate.

We keep paying our debt. We keep applying for lower-interest credit cards. We don't make credit card purchases. We check our credit reports (we can get these for free when we're denied credit) to make sure they're accurate. One glorious day we'll cross the line. We'll pay less interest. We'll speed up the rate at which we get out of debt.

**Today I will renew my determination
to be free of unsecured debt.**

◆　◆　◆

October 7

Now the alternative to despair is courage.
And human life can be viewed as a continuous struggle
between these two options. Courage is the capacity to
affirm one's life in spite of the elements which threaten
it. The fact that courage usually predominates over
despair in itself tells us something important about life.
It tells you that the forces that affirm life are stronger
than those that negate it.

—PAUL E. PFUETZE

❖ ❖ ❖

Being in debt can lead us into a depression. Likewise,
being depressed can lead us into debt as we gamble
or spend to escape the feelings. Having low energy, losing sleep, oversleeping, losing weight, gaining weight,
not enjoying the pleasures in life, and having suicidal
thoughts are signs of depression. If we feel this way for
weeks at a time, we may have a depressive disorder that
needs to be treated with counseling and medication.

Taking that first step to get help is the hardest. Our
egos try to convince us that nothing will help and that
no one will understand. We don't want to see ourselves
as being weak or helpless; we want to be strong and
overcome this ourselves. We find the courage to take
the first step, and we do it now.

Today I will act with courage.

❖ ❖ ❖

October 8

Words pay no debt.

—WILLIAM SHAKESPEARE

❖ ❖ ❖

We acknowledge that our goal is to stop incurring and to pay off unsecured debt. But what happens when there's an emergency? We may have just put ourselves on a spending plan and not accrued enough savings to fix our broken car. We've cut up all our credit cards. Now what do we do?

We remember that the difference between unsecured debt and secured debt is collateral. If we need to borrow $150 from a friend to fix our car, we offer something in exchange. It could be a band instrument, a pair of skis, a coin collection, or a VCR. We don't use our collateral to justify unnecessary spending. We use it for emergencies. We get creative and willing. In our willingness to make good on our debt we feel a sense of pride, rather than a sense of lack.

**Today I will consider what possessions
I could use as collateral in an emergency.**

❖ ❖ ❖

October 9

[Suicide is] the severest form of self-criticism.

—LEONARD LEVINSON

◆ ◆ ◆

When we feel hopeless and despondent, suicide can seem like the best, the easiest, and the fastest solution.

If we're feeling hopeless and despondent because of our financial situation or an addiction or both, we need to get help. Suicidal thoughts are more common than we might expect. Those who live to tell about their thoughts will tell us how grateful they are for getting through—rather than abruptly ending—the pain. In retrospect, they realize that no loss or pain is worth ending our lives over.

We think it through. Our religious beliefs may tell us that suicide is a sin, that our souls will suffer in purgatory. Or maybe we believe in reincarnation and envision coming back into this world only to have to repeat the pain—to get through the lesson—so that we learn what our Higher Power has put us here to learn.

Today I will know in my heart that
life gets better; life can be cherished.
The deeper my pain the greater the joy to come.

◆ ◆ ◆

October 10

Money may not buy happiness, but it can
buy the type of misery you can live with.

—ZIGGY

◆ ◆ ◆

We think to ourselves, "Wouldn't it be nice not to
have to worry about the washer breaking down?"
"Wouldn't it be nice to drive a reliable car?" "Wouldn't
it be nice to take a Caribbean vacation every year?"
"Wouldn't it be nice not to have to work?" If we had
money, we think, at least we wouldn't have to worry
so much and could live comfortably.

True. Money buys external comfort—plush couches
and chairs, luxury cars, beautiful environments. Money
buys what comforts and soothes us on the outside. And,
if we're going to be miserable anyway, why not do it
in comfort?

We remember that regardless of our surroundings,
misery is misery. Unless we have the right attitude, we'll
find something wrong with whatever we have or don't
have. When we work on improving our inner world—
on alleviating the real cause of our misery—we know
true comfort. We know serenity.

**Today I know that the better
I get the richer I become.**

◆ ◆ ◆

October 11

Courage is the power to let go of the familiar.

—RAYMOND LINDQUIST

◆ ◆ ◆

Coeur is the French word for "heart." When we act with courage, we act from our hearts, not our heads alone. We boldly do what feels right. We may be scared if we're going against the grain, but we have confidence and faith supporting our actions.

Being courageous does not require going into battle. We do not have to be saving someone's life. It takes a lot of courage just to be honest with ourselves and others, to decide to change behaviors, and to leave destructive relationships.

Today I will pray for courage.

◆ ◆ ◆

October 12

The cause is hidden, but the result is known.

—OVID

◆ ◆ ◆

We know it's coming before we do it. Our boyfriend dumps us and we devour the ice cream. We don't get the promotion so we head for the bar. We have a fight with our spouse and treat ourselves to a new leather jacket—at his or her expense. We decide that because we're feeling bad anyway, we might as well take full advantage of it. We figure the worse we feel, the more entitled we are to the indulgence.

This type of behavior starts a cycle. The worse we feel, the more we want to self-destruct. Let's face it, our actions are usually premeditated. We think about the ice cream, the drink, or the leather jacket until we can get to it. During the planning stage, we can shift gears. We think it through. We know we have a choice. We decide to do something healthy instead of destructive.

Today I will make only healthy choices for myself.

◆ ◆ ◆

October 13

Between saying and doing,
many a pair of shoes are worn out.

—ITALIAN PROVERB

◆ ◆ ◆

We keep saying we don't like being in debt, but we don't do anything about it. We either don't know where to start or we don't feel like starting.

If we want our circumstances to change, we must be proactive and do the changing. We could waste our lives waiting around for an outside force to save us or get us moving, but only we are responsible for our behavior and our happiness. If we've worn out our shoes doing nothing and going nowhere, we don't go out and buy a new pair of shoes so we can start over again. We stop waiting for a savior. We help ourselves.

**Today I will ask my Higher Power for
the strength and courage to help myself.**

◆ ◆ ◆

October 14

If you want a place in the sun, you must
leave the shade of the family tree.

—OSAGE PROVERB

◆　◆　◆

Some of us have parents who always come to our res-
cue, offering to buy us clothes, to pay our car insurance, or to give us a down payment for a home. They're
willing to help us in any way they can; they only want
the best for us.

When parents or others give us money, they may
have the best intentions. Some parents—whether consciously or subconsciously—think that by providing for
us into adulthood, they can continue to have a say in
what we do and don't do.

We graciously decline bailouts. We let our parents
know that we appreciate the offers but we're getting our
lives under control. We feel the freedom. Our parents
learn to let go.

**Today I will know that accepting
bailouts actually keeps me in debt.**

◆　◆　◆

October 15

Debt takes away options. If you run up debts today
with the thought that you'll pay for all that stuff later,
you're doing more than deferring payment. You're
giving up options in the months and years to come.

—MARY HUNT

◆ ◆ ◆

Zero interest for six months and zero down payment."
These ads are tempting. How can we lose? We
decide we need to have the new carpeting now so that
the house will look great for the holidays. Or we think
that our spouse has had a tough year. We'll get her some
fine jewelry. We'll have six months to come up with the
money.

"Zero interest" ads are meant to get us to spend more
than we typically would. "Zero interest" puts us in
denial. We think we'll come up with the money, but six
months goes by awfully fast. Before we know it, July is
here and we're paying the 25 percent interest rate we
blindly agreed to in December. We didn't come out
ahead, and we're deeper in debt, canceling out any
progress we may have made and instead choosing to
keep ourselves in debt for years to come.

Today I will think it through.

◆ ◆ ◆

October 16

Do what you can, with what you have, where you are.

—THEODORE ROOSEVELT

◆　◆　◆

If we're new to the concept of getting out of debt by not debting one day at a time, we may not have any cash stored away specifically for the holiday season. Even if we've been doing this for a while, we may have underestimated the amount of cash we'd actually need. Because we need this money rather quickly, we get creative about where we can find it.

Mary Hunt, in *Debt-Proof Your Holidays,* suggests many preholiday tips: don't spend coins; temporarily cut back on grocery spending for a couple of months by using up what's in the house; save the "extra" check you receive in October (if you're paid biweekly); work some overtime or take on a part-time job.

**Today I will brainstorm about how
I can "crash" save for the holidays.**

◆　◆　◆

October 17

Sleep is to strain and purify the emotions,
to deposit the mud of life, to calm the fever of
the soul, to return into the bosom of material
nature . . . a sort of innocence and purification.

—HENRY F. AMIEL

◆　◆　◆

Worrying about money can keep us up at night. The next day we feel a bit fatigued, stressed, and anxious. If we experience more restless nights, our days become overwhelming. We feel worn and tense. We don't think straight. We don't take the energy to eat right. Nothing feels right. Basically, we don't know what we're doing. We're frustrated. Without enough sleep, we carry around "the mud of life."

Getting a good night's rest is a basic physical, mental, emotional, and spiritual need. Without it, we go nowhere fast. With it, we're in a place to make the best choices. We make getting enough rest our number one priority. We discuss our problem with another, whether a spouse, friend, clergy, therapist, or physician. We simplify our life as much as possible until we're back on track. We learn whatever we can about achieving a good night's sleep.

**Today I will accept that getting
enough rest needs to be a top priority.**

◆　◆　◆

October 18

Spirituality is invisible. Never forget that. If you
can see it, if it's dressed in funny robes, if it's up there
to be looked at, if it's making a big performance
of itself, it is not spirituality. It is ego.

—STUART WILDE

◆　◆　◆

When some of us experience spiritual awakenings
or paradigm shifts, we may go through an awkward stage. We've learned some wonderful things and
we want to share them, but we don't pull it off very elegantly. We try to help a friend in need but end up convincing our friend only that we've "changed."

We can't see spirituality, but we know spirituality
when we see it. Spiritual people are usually content,
confident, present, hopeful, positive, lighthearted, open,
and—often—silent. We don't hear them boasting about
meditating or see them pushing someone to join a spiritual group. They don't feel a need to prove anything or
to show the world what they know.

We share our spiritual knowledge in bits and pieces.
We learn to sense when someone's ready to hear what
we have to say. Until then, we remain silent.

**Today I will know that I sometimes
help others most by just being.**

◆　◆　◆

October 19

Somewhere along the line in my journey
to solvency I made a profound, life-changing discovery.
I learned that I could replace my fear of deprivation
with the joy of sacrifice.

—MARY HUNT

◆　◆　◆

Deprivation means having something we enjoy taken away. *Sacrifice,* on the other hand, means to give up something we value so that we can replace it with something that's become even more valuable to us. Deprivation is depressing. With deprivation, we lose some power. Sacrifice, however, is admirable. It is a worthy cause. It has a beauty to it.

We return to our values. Do we value financial freedom? A debt-free life? Is that value more important than a new computer or new clothes?

Today I will sacrifice for my own good.

◆　◆　◆

October 20

One cannot defend production as satisfying wants
if that production creates the wants. . . .
Production only fills a void that it has itself created.

—JOHN KENNETH GALBRAITH

◆ ◆ ◆

Most of us don't wake up every day wanting a material object that doesn't exist. Before CD players, VCRs, microwave ovens, and cell phones existed, we most likely didn't desire them. We may have wished for an invention to make cooking easier, but unless a microwave oven existed in our minds, there was no void to fill.

When we desire what is put in front of us, we feel inclined to fill a void that didn't before exist. Before making a purchase, we're wise to question whether we're filling our own void or the void created by an industry. We have enough personal voids to fill without wasting time on filling those created for us by someone or something else.

**Today I will concentrate on filling any emptiness
I feel on the inside—not the outside.**

◆ ◆ ◆

October 21

Madness is often the logic of
an accurate mind overtaxed.

—OLIVER WENDELL HOLMES

◆　◆　◆

Addictive behavior can leave family members feeling betrayed. In the end, it's not that our gambling husband can't provide us with a nice home and car. When lies, deception, and manipulation run rampant in a relationship, we are confused. We question our memory; we question what's real and what's imaginary—we question our sanity. We check out. We don't know what to do or where to go for help. We don't believe help exists.

When we get to a point where we question our sanity (or preferably before that point), when we feel we're going to have a nervous breakdown, we step away from the madness. Someway, somehow, we find the means. We take a leave of absence from work. We stay with relatives. We physically remove ourselves from the insanity so that we may distance ourselves emotionally and mentally as well. With distance, we get clarity. With clarity, we know what is real.

Today I will force myself to take necessary breaks.

◆　◆　◆

October 22

Perseverance is patience concentrated.
—THOMAS CARLYLE

❖ ❖ ❖

Some of us have healthy spending patterns. We take responsibility for our happiness and our behavior, yet we wake up one day deep in debt.

Debt can happen to anyone at any time; it knows no boundaries. Security is no guarantee. We may have become chronically ill, have suffered an unexpected investment loss, or lost property from a natural disaster. Whatever the reason, we suddenly find ourselves in this strange and uncomfortable place called debt.

We may panic. We've never been here before. How can we get out of this? We may be angry, feeling that something has in effect been stolen from us. Is this how our Higher Power rewards our responsibility?

We already possess many of the coping skills we need to get through our debt. We focus on getting through our feelings. We know that we are not alone. We find support from people in similar circumstances. Also, we ponder the strange turn of events. We look for the lesson we can learn from our circumstances.

**Today I will pray for the strength
to start over again.**

❖ ❖ ❖

October 23

The road to Hell is paved with good intentions.
—SAMUEL JOHNSON

◆ ◆ ◆

Depending on the reason for our debt, some people may feel sorry for us. They know we're doing our best to get by. They know we're having a tough time making ends meet. They know we're good people with good intentions. They know we deserve to be paid more. They only want the best for us.

People who feel sorry for us often try to pick up the tab. They buy gifts for us but won't accept any in return. They don't ask us for donations when they're fund-raising. They have hearts of gold and good intentions. The problem can be, especially for those of us who are prone to leaning on others till they fall over, that we tend to absorb their projection of us—we're poor, needy people who can't take care of ourselves.

We graciously accept what others want to give to us, but we are firm about what we're able to do for ourselves. We also make a point to give—somehow, some way—in return. In doing so, we affirm to ourselves and others that we're willing and able to meet our responsibilities.

Today I will feel confident about my ability to take responsibility.

◆ ◆ ◆

October 24

Responsibility is the great developer.
—Louis D. Brandeis

◆ ◆ ◆

We're all in debt for different reasons. Some of us spend more than we have; some of us live with people who spend more than we have.

Before we enact a spending plan that involves trying to earn more money, we need to ask ourselves some key questions. The primary question is, Who is responsible for the debt? If we aren't, we need to ask ourselves why we're taking on a second job, agreeing to do extra projects, or looking for a new job. We also ask ourselves whether the person responsible for the debt is still debting. If the answer is yes, we question whether bringing home more money will improve our situation.

**Today, before I agree to do more work,
I will put my circumstances into perspective.**

◆ ◆ ◆

October 25

You can complain because roses have thorns,
or you can rejoice because thorns have roses.

—ZIGGY

◆　◆　◆

For some of us the challenge lies in finding ways to earn more money. This can feel like a constant struggle or burden. Our goal may be to find a job that pays more. But, in the meantime, if we find ourselves taking on a second job, working extra hours, or taking on special projects, we may get overtired and over-stressed.

We remind ourselves that these circumstances are temporary. We step up to the plate. Complaining and wishing things were different takes us out of the present moment. We miss the opportunity to grow from our challenge. If we dedicate ourselves to using our extra earnings to pay our bills, our debts decrease. The amount of interest paid each month on credit cards declines. As long as we are not continuing to debt or living with a compulsive debtor (in which case we're better off not working extra), we see progress. Our situation is not forever.

Today I will know that the positive choices I make now will bring positive results in the days to come.

◆　◆　◆

October 26

Just about the time you think you can make
both ends meet, somebody moves the ends.

—PANSY PENNER

◆　◆　◆

Our spending plan has been working swimmingly
for quite some time now. We're feeling confident.
But as much as we plan and prepare to meet our present and future financial obligations, we're bound to run
into the unexpected—the event or circumstance that
throws a wrench into our plans. We lose our job, get
ill, get robbed. Whether big or small, the setback is
enough to make us angry.

Instead of looking back with anger, we accept that
the unexpected is part of life; it's something we have
no control over. It may feel like we're being pushed
backward, yet a setback can actually move us forward.
If we're being evicted from our apartment because the
building has been sold, maybe it's time we moved on
anyway.

We take on the challenge with a can-do attitude. We
revisit our spending plan and our contingency account.
We get creative. We've already affirmed that we can get
out of debt—nothing is going to stop us now. We use
all the skills we acquired when we first took action to
get out of debt.

Today I will look for the good in the unexpected.

◆　◆　◆

October 27

It is a bad plan that admits of no modification.

—PUBLILIUS SYRUS

◆　◆　◆

We think we've got it all figured out. We're working our spending plan. We know how much money is coming in and going out. We know what we're saving for, and we have a stash set aside for emergencies. We're feeling good. Everything is under control.

Then something simple happens, and we get all out of whack. A birthday or rebate check for three hundred dollars arrives in the mail. We hadn't expected it. It's not in our plan, and so we get confused. Do we revise our spending plan? Buy some clothes? Pay more toward a bill? Treat some friends to a night on the town?

Our spending plan is a tool to keep us on track—to help us reach our goal of getting out of debt. Our spending plan is a guidepost, not a brain. We don't have to feel guilty for wanting to spend the money. We put the money in our savings account until we decide where or whether to spend it.

**Today I will consider how much
power I've given my spending plan.**

◆　◆　◆

October 28

Find a job you like and you
add five days to every week.
—H. JACKSON BROWNE

◆ ◆ ◆

Each of us has a calling in life. Each of us does something, in our own way, better than anyone else on the planet. If and when we discover our calling, we know it. We love what we're doing, no matter how hard we have to work. We don't look at the clock to see when it's time to leave; we glance out the window and notice the sun has already set.

Some of us may miss our calling because we get too focused on money. We want our million in the bank—our "two commas." We look at a job or career and consider how much it pays. Certainly, compensation is a strong consideration. But when we choose to do what we love—to develop a career based on our aspirations, on what beckons us—we find our calling. And when we find our calling, somehow, *all* our needs are met.

**Today I will make a list of the things I love
to do and will try to piece it into a career.**

◆ ◆ ◆

October 29

When you really want love,
you will find it waiting for you.
—OSCAR WILDE

◆ ◆ ◆

Some of us are always searching. We never seem to find what we're looking for. We convince ourselves that a big home and a fast car hold the answers. While big homes and fast cars can be nice things to have, they won't make us complete. Completeness comes from loving ourselves unconditionally and from being able to love others the same way—unconditionally, without expectations, without being needy.

Love heals. When we love ourselves and others unconditionally, we heal ourselves and others. When unconditional love is behind our intentions, we can move mountains. There's nothing more powerful.

Today I will not place any conditions
on myself or others. I will love myself
and others just the way we are. I will
experience the power of unconditional love.

◆ ◆ ◆

October 30

The only thing we have to fear is fear itself.
—FRANKLIN D. ROOSEVELT

◆　◆　◆

Burying ourselves in negative thoughts and self-doubt, feeling needy and insecure, clamoring for affection or compassion, making others feel inadequate, standing frozen in our tracks—these are all signs of fear.

When we act this way, we ask ourselves why we can't move beyond these feelings. Are we afraid of losing key material goods, our popularity, our money, or our pride? Are we afraid that if we don't have money our spouse will leave, our friends will abandon us, and people will see us not as achievers but as losers? Are we afraid of being alone? Humiliated?

**Today I will ask myself what
keeps me from moving forward.**

◆　◆　◆

October 31

Fear is that little darkroom
where negatives are developed.
—MICHAEL PRITCHARD

* * *

One dictionary defines *fear* as "an unpleasant often strong emotion caused by anticipation or awareness of danger." How we define *danger* is, of course, very personal. What frightens one person may not phase another. But we all know the feeling. We've all had it at one point or another. Some of us live with it. What's for certain is that fear can keep us from accomplishing some important financial and other goals.

We're told we need to face our fears. What exactly does that mean? How exactly is that done? First we identify a fear. Then we silently acknowledge and honor it. We tell it we know why it is there. We send it positive, loving energy and thoughts of peace and goodwill. Each time we do this, the fear slowly subsides. We know what is true. We know what is important.

Today I will acknowledge one fear.

* * *

November 1

When I loan someone money,
I never expect to get it back.
—REBECCA POST

◆ ◆ ◆

Most of us have a policy about lending money to people or about co-signing loans. Some of us never lend money to anyone. At the other extreme, some of us are quite free with our money, whether we have it or not. Most of us, though, are in-between. We weigh the consequences, consider the amount of money and who it is we're lending money to, and decide whether it's a worthy cause. Sometimes we get our money back with interest. In many cases, we never see it again or for years to come. If that happens, we may feel resentful, and a close relationship could be at stake.

We consider the concept of lending money under the assumption that we'll never get it back. If we're comfortable with that, we lend the money. If we're not, either we don't make the loan or we create a contract with terms. Putting something down on paper solidifies the deal.

**Today I will review my past
experiences with lending money.**

◆ ◆ ◆

November 2

> The price we pay when pursuing any art or
> calling is an intimate knowledge of its ugly side.
>
> —JAMES BALDWIN

◆　◆　◆

We long for a higher-paying job to pay off our debt, for more fulfilling relationships, or for good health. We envision how wonderful everything would be. When we're "ready," we may get exactly what we wished and prayed for. At that moment, we need to be ready for the side effects. These are the consequences we hadn't thought of that are likely to cause some grief: We make more money, but we're far busier than we want to be; we've paid off our debt but now our children are asking to borrow lots of money from us; we have a new romance, but our partner takes up all of our free time.

Life is a double-edged sword. Along with our treasured dreams comes the inevitable downside. We trust that the price is worth it. We know that by following our desires we reach a place where we're supposed to be. We meet the new challenges.

Today I will accept the "good" with the "bad."

◆　◆　◆

November 3

Meditation is really the practice of allowing yourself to just be and being comfortable with *whatever* comes up.

—JON KABAT-ZINN

❖　❖　❖

We wash dishes and think of bills to pay. We drive to work and dwell over how little we make. We lie in bed and think about how nobody cares to hear about our chronic pain or about losing so much money at the casino. Our mind is not where we are—ever. It's constantly someplace else.

Mindfulness is the meditative practice of being present and aware in every moment; not of clearing the mind, as if we were in a deep meditative state, but of giving our attention to our breath, to where we are, and to what we're doing at the time. We live each moment as if it were our last. We give each moment the respect, attention, and awareness it deserves.

**Today I will treat every moment
as if it were sacred.**

❖　❖　❖

November 4

Once you free your notion of self-worth from the bonds of material things, you will need less and you will spend less. As your self-esteem rises, your debt will diminish. Call it a law of financial physics.

—SUZE ORMAN

◆　◆　◆

We may buy or spend not to *have* more but to *be* more. We feel bad about ourselves and create a Catch-22. We feel inadequate, we spend to feel better, and we then feel bad for spending. The negative feelings linger and worsen; the debt increases.

We can choose to look at ourselves as lacking and keep ourselves in the cycle of debt. Or we can believe we're already fully developed inside. What we really need to do is shed the fears and negative beliefs that keep us from reaching our potential. The more we shed, the more we expose of our true (and completely adequate) selves.

Today I will see myself as being fully equipped. I have within me everything I will ever need.

◆　◆　◆

November 5

Harmony exists in difference no less than in likeness,
if only the same keynote governs both parts.

—MARGARET FULLER

◆　◆　◆

Our partner may take a completely different view of money than we do. Just when we think we're getting ahead, she takes a month off work to retreat. Or perhaps our partner puts us on a tight budget and goes ballistic when we spend more than he thinks is appropriate.

We remember that we are a team. The keynote that governs us is the quality of our relationship with each other—how much time and effort we put into making the relationship work and whether we're open to learning new relationship skills.

It's our attitude—not necessarily our partner's actions—that can create disharmony. When the actions interfere with fundamental aspects of our relationship, such as trust and intimacy, we question whether our spouse has the quality of our relationship in mind. If not, we need to address marital issues and possible addiction. Otherwise, we remember that we are all individuals with unique needs. We are different and that's part of why we're together.

**Today I will know that
deep down we are all free spirits.**

◆　◆　◆

November 6

You create your reality with your intention.
—GARY ZUKOV

◆　◆　◆

Some days all we can think about is what's wrong in our lives. We never have money, we need a new car, or another bill is past due. We attract what we focus on. When we think negative thoughts and feel negative feelings, we create negativity.

The opposite is also true. When we think positive thoughts and feel positive feelings, we create positive change in our lives.

Today I will focus on what I want, not on what I don't have. I will pray that my desires are in accordance with the highest good for me and all life everywhere.

◆　◆　◆

November 7

There is no chance, no destiny, no fate,
that can circumvent or hinder or control
the firm resolve of a determined soul.

—ELLA WHEELER WILCOX

◆　◆　◆

Day and night we think about our money problems. When we manage to forget for a few moments, the phone rings and it's a creditor, or we go to the mailbox only to find another overdraft notice. Our thoughts return to our debt. All our energy, all our attention, goes toward this big huge negative obstacle, these numbers we call debt. We obsess.

Obsession can be closely linked to passion. It's basically the same kind of energy, only when we're being passionate, we direct our thoughts and feelings toward something we want—toward something positive.

**Today I will turn my obsession into
my passion by aiming for the positive.**

◆　◆　◆

November 8

Self-respect is to be mentally faithful to yourself.

—ANONYMOUS

◆ ◆ ◆

Low self-esteem can create a need to underearn or to seek material goods as compensation. Because money is so closely related to self-esteem for many of us, being in debt—regardless of the reason—can reinforce feelings of worthlessness. We feel "less than" others. We question our abilities. We compare ourselves with others. We become insecure, a feeling that gets reinforced over and over again.

We remember that we are where we need to be in life. We are children of God. How could we be "less than"? We respect our feelings of hopelessness and insecurity, knowing they are part of us. We respect the power we hold within to overcome.

Today I will treat myself with respect.

◆ ◆ ◆

November 9

No problem is too big to run away from.
—AL RIES AND JACK TROUT

◆ ◆ ◆

Fear of impending or endless debt rings a bell for many—but not all—people. Some of us still cringe when we think of the forty dollars we lost in Las Vegas three years ago. Those of us who spend or gamble compulsively are so caught up in the action or in escaping that we lose all sense of money, just as people lose sense of time. Spending a thousand dollars at the blackjack table or through a home shopping network inflicts no pain on us while we're doing it, but sooner or later the pain catches up to us.

We hear about alcoholics and addicts reaching rock bottom. Life has gotten so out of control that they make a choice to change. They've reached their lowest low. Now it's time to pick themselves up and move forward. The same can be said for debtors. We all have a low point, and it is different for everyone. We know it when we get there. We know when we need to change.

Today I will remind myself that hitting rock bottom means a miracle is about to take place.

◆ ◆ ◆

November 10

To command is to serve, nothing more and nothing less.

—ANDRÉ MALRAUX

◆　◆　◆

We may have agreed with our partner that one person handles the bookkeeping—pays all bills, keeps track of paperwork, monitors financial statements, and balances the checkbook. While this method may work extremely well for some couples, if the chosen bookkeeper starts keeping secrets, it can be a great source of strife.

Either partner, whether bringing home a paycheck or not, is entitled to know where family finances stand—how much money is coming in, where it's going, and how discretionary income is being divided. The "silent" partner also needs to have an equal say in family financial goals.

Today I will practice honesty in all my affairs.

◆　◆　◆

November 11

One by one, we can rechoose—to awaken. To leave the prison of our conditioning, to love, to turn homeward.

—MARILYN FERGUSON

◆ ◆ ◆

If our spouse refuses to seek help for a drinking, drugging, gambling, or compulsive spending problem, we may reach a point where we consider leaving. The rage, the isolation, and the numbness of feelings drag us down to extremely unhealthy emotional, physical, mental, and spiritual levels.

Rather than waiting until the addict reaches rock bottom, we take care of ourselves. In that way, we are in a better position to give healthy support and to take care of other family members, especially children.

Today I will make a call to discuss my situation with someone supportive— a friend, family member, or therapist.

◆ ◆ ◆

November 12

The curious paradox is that when I accept myself
just as I am, then I can change.
—CARL ROGERS

◆ ◆ ◆

After months or years of fear, anger, confusion, or
rage over finances, we reach a point where we feel
at peace. Not just for a day or two, or even a week, but
for much longer. We face a painful event and notice our
reaction isn't what it would have been a year ago. That
growth is so incredibly soothing and refreshing. It's not
just a good day; it's a wonderful life.

We know we've learned some new coping skills. We
make a point to remember what keeps us serene. We
may slip every now and then, but we can fall back on
our new coping skills. There will be a time when we
grow again. For now, we enjoy our newfound serenity.

**Today I will know that emotional
stability is mine to keep.**

◆ ◆ ◆

November 13

Oh, grow up.

—JOAN RIVERS

◆　◆　◆

For the most part, being a kid can be a great thing. As young children, we let our parents or guardians worry about bills, food, clothing, and shelter. We may not have liked everything we ate and we may have complained about what we had to wear, but we didn't *worry* about it. It wasn't our responsibility.

Some of us are in debt because we haven't grown up yet. We still don't see a need to concentrate on earning or saving money to meet our needs. We still want to play, only now our playgrounds are casinos or shopping malls. We turn to parents, siblings, the government—whoever we think can cover for us.

Today I will imagine how I would react if others expected from me what I expect from them.

◆　◆　◆

November 14

I'm good enough, I'm smart enough,
and doggone it, people like me.
—STUART SMALLEY

❖   ❖   ❖

Research has proven that our thoughts, over time, can actually alter our brain chemistry and determine how many mood-enhancing neurotransmitters (such as endorphins, serotonin, and dopamine) our brain releases. If we're always thinking negative thoughts about ourselves and others, our brains get accustomed to releasing fewer mood-enhancing neurotransmitters. We in effect bring ourselves down.

The opposite is also true. If we think positive thoughts about ourselves and others and are optimistic, our brain chemistry improves. Thinking good things about ourselves means accepting ourselves, flaws and all.

Today, and every day for the next six months, I will look in the mirror and tell myself I'm okay.

❖   ❖   ❖

November 15

Imagination is more important than knowledge.
Knowledge is limited. Imagination encircles the world.

—ALBERT EINSTEIN

◆　◆　◆

When we're in debt, we tend to view money as a restriction. We can't do this or that because we don't have enough money. Our perspective is, "I'll never have enough."

We open our minds to new ways of thinking. We look at money as being elastic. We can stretch it, shape it, mold it into what we want. We are the boss of the money; it is not the boss of us. We are choosing what to do with our money. We can put ourselves on an inflexible budget or a flexible spending plan. We can be rigid in our expectations of ourselves, or we can cut ourselves a bit of slack.

**Today I will decide who is in charge—
me or my money.**

◆　◆　◆

November 16

Many an opportunity is lost because
a man is out looking for four-leaf clovers.

—Anonymous

◆ ◆ ◆

When we call ourselves lucky, it's usually because we receive some good fortune we either didn't expect or got by the skin of our teeth. But luck doesn't usually just happen. Luck is when preparation meets opportunity. We know what we want from life, and we prepare for it by learning a new skill or dealing with a problem. Then, when conditions are ripe, an opportunity presents itself. If we take it, we call ourselves lucky, or the recipient of a miracle.

Many of us have turned this around. Instead of preparing for the good things we want, we go out looking for them: a big win at the casino or the highest-paying job we can find. When our four-leaf clovers come to us, we're unprepared and cannot take the opportunities. We miss out because we're looking at the prize and avoiding the process.

**Today I will trust that my Higher Power
brings forth what I am prepared to receive.**

◆ ◆ ◆

November 17

I have to remember that the people
on top of the mountain didn't fall there.

—SARA T.

◆　◆　◆

The feelings of discomfort seem to come out of the blue. We're minding our own business when a friend calls and tells us about the great new job she landed, and we start to feel envious. We're at a house-warming party and all of a sudden we're no longer enjoying ourselves. We regret that our house is not as beautiful.

When we compare ourselves to others, we're feeling inadequate, insecure, and envious all at once. We long for what someone else has or does, and the clincher is that we don't believe we're capable of having or doing it.

We pay attention to what we tend to compare. The comparisons usually involve aspects about ourselves that we feel are inadequate. It may be about money, possessions, body image, or relationships. Our comparisons reveal some of our deepest needs.

Today I will think of what action steps I can take
to accept what I have and then to get what I want.

◆　◆　◆

November 18

What we give to the poor . . . is what
we carry with us when we die.

—PETER MARTIN

◆　◆　◆

We've established that it's vitally important to take care of ourselves, to make self-care our number one priority. We know that when we do so, all else falls into place. Part of self-care is allowing ourselves to help others in a healthy way. This doesn't mean being there to bail out an addict, which is the opposite of support. It means making a positive difference by donating money, items, or time to an organization or cause we believe in.

When we adopt a giving mentality, we feel abundance. We know in our hearts that we'll have what we need because whatever we give, willingly and effortlessly, we will receive in kind. We feel the joy from giving with an open heart rather than the fear and insecurity of clinging to our money, possessions, and time. We're taking care of ourselves.

**Today I will determine what percentage
of my income I will donate, what possessions
I can give away, or how I can volunteer my time.**

◆　◆　◆

November 19

There is nothing either good or bad,
but thinking makes it so.

—WILLIAM SHAKESPEARE

◆   ◆   ◆

If we smoke, we're well aware of how much money we spend every week buying cigarettes. We're also most likely fed up with the grief we get in public. We may tell ourselves we want to continue smoking just because it's our right to choose. In truth, research has proven nicotine to be one of the most addictive drugs available. Although nicotine isn't very potent, its addictive qualities are more powerful than those of heroin or cocaine.

We remember two of the goals on every debtor's list: to cut back on expenses and to take care of our health as best we can to prevent illness. We accept that quitting smoking is a step in the right direction. We quit smoking for ourselves, our families, and our financial future.

**Today I will explore the different methods
available to help me quit smoking.**

◆   ◆   ◆

November 20

Assumptions allow the best in life to pass you by.
—JOHN SALES

◆　◆　◆

Planning for expected expenses is easy enough. We know roughly how much the monthly phone, electric, and gas bills are going to be. We know how much rent or mortgage money to set aside, and we can get a good sense of monthly grocery, clothing, and entertainment expenses. If we give these spending categories even the least bit of attention, they're not surprises.

Somehow, though, many of us manage to forget to plan for expenses that crop up every few months or once or twice a year. Car insurance, car repair, vacations, pet expenses, birthdays, Christmas, and other celebrations. We know they're coming. They aren't secrets. Yet we're inclined to put them on the back burner. "We'll deal with them when they get here," we think. "We'll be in a better financial position at that point." We assume that we'll be able to manage them at a later date.

Today I will prepare for the inevitable.

◆　◆　◆

November 21

You love me so much, you want to put me in your pocket. And I should die there smothered.

—D. H. LAWRENCE

◆ ◆ ◆

We do it all in the name of love. Our spouse gambles or drinks too much, or maybe both. We love our spouse so much, we love the thought of what our lives could be together, that we end up trying our damnedest to rectify what we see as a bad situation. To gain control over something we know deep down we're powerless over, we yell, cry, complain, ignore, and pout—anything to get his or her attention. Anything to get him or her to change.

In the process of trying to change someone to be what we want them to be—to put them in our pockets so we can control their every move—we push him or her away from us. In our minds, we're trying to make things right. In the eyes of those we're trying to change, we're lunatics. So much of our attention is focused on someone else's behavior that we forget who we are. We're no longer bringing ourselves into the relationship.

Today I will concentrate on changing me.

◆ ◆ ◆

November 22

Gratitude is a blessing we give to one another.
—ROBERT RAYNOLDS

❖ ❖ ❖

Being grateful for the positive aspects of our lives can instantly bring us up when we're feeling down. All we need to do is to take time to find the good in our lives.

Every day, every week, or every month or so, we can sit down and make a list of what we're grateful for. As our minds start rolling, the pen keeps scrolling. We'll be amazed at how long the list can get. When we put it next to a list of what we have to feel bad about we realize how much unwarranted attention and energy we've given to our debt; we see the power of negative thinking, how we let it consume our days, and how it deprives us of enjoying what we have.

Today I will list five things I have to be grateful for.

❖ ❖ ❖

November 23

The manner of giving is worth more than the gift.

—PIERRE CORNEILLE

◆　◆　◆

We know that we have a lot to be grateful for—we've made our lists. We know the importance of giving. We give what we want to receive; we give with open hearts and no regrets. When we combine the two, when we're grateful that we have the ability to give and to help others, we feel a powerful presence. We know we're in tune with the universe and that our Higher Power is with us, working through us.

Regardless of how much debt we carry, we can always give—time, gifts, money, compliments, and good thoughts. We can be grateful that we possess the ability wherever we go.

**Today I will be thankful that
I experience the joy of giving.**

◆　◆　◆

November 24

You can experience a joyful season without mortgaging
your future to pay for a transitory good feeling. You can
become a fully committed no-new-debt, no-way, no-how
kind of person. It's all a matter of attitude—something
over which you have tremendous control.

—MARY HUNT

◆　◆　◆

During the holiday season, we're moved by the
music, the lights, the joy of giving. It appeals to our
senses. We decide that we're in debt anyway, so what
difference does it make if we go deeper? At least we'll
make someone happy with this gift, and our holiday
lights will please passersby. These feelings are strong,
enhanced by the spirit of the holiday season. It's all so
beautiful. We feel a need to be part of it.

When we're absorbed in the magical holiday atmosphere, we lose our sense of money. We want to create
this wonderful *feeling* at home. We spend money based
on our feelings, not our spending plan.

People have been celebrating holidays for centuries,
before there was electricity for light and before there
were ready-made gifts of every shape, size, and color.
We can create the feeling—the spirit of the holidays—
without all the hoopla. If we use our brains and remind
ourselves of our new attitude toward debting, we won't
debt.

**Today I will use my intellect, not my
feelings, when shopping for the holidays.**

◆　◆　◆

November 25

Perhaps I am stronger than I think.

—THOMAS MERTON

◆ ◆ ◆

Almost everyone who walks this earth carries around a certain amount of shame over past behavior. This may be especially true for people with addictions and, on another level, for people who are chronically ill or have lost money in business. We feel ashamed for hurting people, and we carry the shame with us, hurting ourselves.

Shame can paralyze us emotionally. To get beyond the feeling, we go to the source. We make a list of people we've harmed—from spouses to creditors—through our action or inaction. We let them know how we now feel about our past behavior. We show them we recognize that we've caused some serious consequences and are willing to take responsibility. We act with humility and grace. We expect nothing in return. We apologize. By making amends, we release our shame and we no longer put energy into pretending we're not ashamed. We open the door to better relationships and positive behaviors.

Today I will know that my well-being depends in part on how I treat others.

◆ ◆ ◆

November 26

> When I am anxious it is because I am
> living in the future. When I am depressed
> it is because I am living in the past.
>
> —JIMMY R.

◆ ◆ ◆

We're advised to live in the present moment, to live one day at a time. Great advice, but how do we do it?

At the beginning of each day, we take just a couple of minutes to review all (the "good" and the "bad") that we have in our lives—job, family, friends, debt, divorce, illness, addiction. Then we imagine that all of it is only for today. Tomorrow we will magically be someplace else. No tragedy, no harrowing experiences, and no death. We just won't have our life as we know it. How would we treat the kids, our co-workers, parents, friends, strangers, and ourselves? How would our expectations and priorities change?

Today I will feel lightness in knowing that I can create beauty each day by simply being.

◆ ◆ ◆

November 27

Blood is an inheritance, virtue an acquisition.

—MIGUEL DE CERVANTES

◆　◆　◆

Although individuals treat money differently, each generation has a general standard regarding money.

During the Depression, we learned to value each scrap of food. In the post–World War II era, we had plenty but knew not to be wasteful. By the 1970s, we were still living within our means but discovering how much more the world had to offer. In the new millennium, many of us don't think twice about getting whatever we want—and we usually want it now.

Today I will reflect on how my generation and world events have influenced my thoughts about money.

◆　◆　◆

November 28

Opportunity may knock only once,
but temptation leans on the doorbell.

—ANONYMOUS

◆　◆　◆

We have an opportunity. We've made getting out of debt a priority in our lives. Just having this desire gives us the opportunity. For this, we are grateful.

It's all too easy, however, to slip into our old ways of thinking and behaving. Our old spending patterns are all too fresh in our mind. We remember to take this opportunity—this juncture in our lives—to learn and to grow. If we're tempted to turn to our old ways, we're going backward.

Today I will remember that my old thinking and behaviors are a part of my history, not my future.

◆　◆　◆

November 29

Fate is what happens to you
and destiny is what you do with it.
—UNKNOWN

◆　◆　◆

As human beings, we're designed to adapt—to weather, food, and circumstances. When we'd rather adapt to an adverse situation than put energy into seeing and accepting it for what it is, this wonderful survival technique leads to our demise.

There are times when it's far better to lose what we have than to try to adapt to it. We may, for instance, think we're strong enough to put up with our spouse's drinking and drugging problem. And for the most part we are strong enough—and that's the problem. We remember that unless we make some changes, bad situations only get worse.

Today I will listen to my heart.

◆　◆　◆

November 30

Beware of little expenses;
a small leak will sink a great ship.
—BENJAMIN FRANKLIN

◆　◆　◆

Why are we buying something or paying extra for a service? Are we buying something only because it's on sale? If so, do we really need it now or in the next couple of weeks? Are we actually wasting a dollar rather than saving a dollar?

We think twice about impulse buying when we take the time to figure out exactly how much money we make per hour. After we subtract taxes, mileage, day care, and all other job-related expenses, how much are we actually making per hour? If our annual salary is thirty thousand dollars, we may only be bringing home five dollars an hour. Is the pretty notepad that catches our eye at the register worth one hour of our day?

Today, when I feel the impulse to buy or to spend,
I will pause and ask myself why I'm handing over
my hard-earned money so casually.

◆　◆　◆

December 1

Money can come and go, but nothing can touch
the treasure we create in the loving of one another.

—UNKNOWN

♦ ♦ ♦

If the house were on fire, what would we run out the
door with? Would we worry more about the children
or the furniture? Would we grab our wallet, dog, pho-
tographs, or the report we just completed for work?

We need love and loving memories. All else can be
replaced.

**Today I will know that my ability to give
and receive love is the foundation
for all that is worth saving in my life.**

♦ ♦ ♦

December 2

If the holidays for you have become a marathon of
crossing tasks off a "to-do" list and counting the days
until it's over, then I suppose operating efficiently is a
worthy goal. But if you're longing for a meaningful time
of spiritual renewal and joyful interaction with your
family, it is *effectiveness* you should seek.

—MARY HUNT

◆ ◆ ◆

The holiday season can get so busy that we ignore
what it is we need to celebrate. We cancel getting
together with friends, rush through baking, stand impa-
tiently in line at the department store, and fight crowds
in the malls. We do this all in the name of celebration.
In the end, and after having spent much time, energy,
and money, we catch our breath only to find that we
didn't enjoy the season; we just reacted to it.

If we're going through the motions and missing the
spirit of the season, we stop and think about our values. What is it exactly that we're celebrating? What can
we do that aligns with our values? How can we do it
simply?

Today I will accept that adding value to the holiday
season improves my well-being and my pocketbook.

◆ ◆ ◆

December 3

Error is feeling where we ought to think, and thinking
where we ought to feel.
—CHURTON COLLINS

◆ ◆ ◆

Whether spending too much money is an issue for
us or not, most of us at least look twice at special offers to buy one, get one free or cash a check for
$2.99 and be automatically enrolled in a program
where we receive special discounts on select products.

We're sometimes drawn to these advertisements,
thinking we'll "save" money. "Think" is the operative
word here. The only reason to pay any attention to
these ads is if we truly are saving money. We question
the ads; we question our needs. We question what we're
committing ourselves to. Do we need to make the purchase? Does it align with our priorities? Are we having
to spend money with the promise of future savings on
other products? Can we live without it? Are we helping anyone?

Today I will review my list of goals and priorities
as a reminder of where I'll allow my dollars to go.

◆ ◆ ◆

December 4

I release my old habit of hasty decision-making
and allow my decisions to evolve and emerge
in harmony with my Higher Power's time.

—MAUREEN BRADY

◆ ◆ ◆

When something breaks, we're tempted to think we
need a new one, or when we see a new gizmo,
we think, "This thing will make my life so much easier!"
It's important to alter our thought pattern. We ask ourselves, Can I fix the broken object? What do I have that
I can use instead? Will I really use the small appliance
regularly? Do I really need another sweater, just
because it's on sale? Can I borrow that power tool?

We then turn our attention to our feelings. Do we feel
gratified, empowered, and maybe even relieved that
we don't need to make a purchase? Are we making a
rational choice that's right for us? We may indeed
need to replace the vacuum cleaner, but do we need
the best?

Through experience, we learn to identify what our
feelings are telling us. If we buy the small appliance and
soon regret it, we remember the feeling we had at the
time of purchase and store it in our memories for later
reference. If we don't purchase and find ourselves truly
needing to go back for something worthwhile, we register that feeling, too.

**Today I will pay close attention to my feelings
when considering or making any purchase.**

◆ ◆ ◆

December 5

Who loves ya, baby?

—TELLY SAVALAS

◆　◆　◆

We love to go shopping for gifts, whether for an occasion or not. We never forget birthdays or anniversaries. If our co-worker gets a promotion, we give her a nice gift. If our best friend is going through a hard time, we buy a small token to show we care. We love having people over to show them a good time, to share our riches with them. We always pick up the tab.

Giving, caring, and thoughtfulness are wonderful qualities. When we're deep in debt yet lavish others with gifts, we question what we're really buying. Are we buying gifts or are we buying love? We trust that our friends and family love us regardless of what we provide them with materially. We still give. We give our time and attention. We give good thoughts.

**Today I will affirm that I am
love and that I am loved.**

◆　◆　◆

December 6

There is one god and he has one thousand faces.

—ANONYMOUS

◆ ◆ ◆

Surveys show that most of us believe in a God. Some of us have a close relationship with our God. Some of us just believe it's out there and leave it at that. Still there are many of us who feel no connection to a God. We may believe that God exists, yet we do not feel the love or guidance. Others do not believe God exists.

Some of us don't have a name for our God. We simply believe in a force or Power greater than ourselves. This could mean the ether in the universe or another unseen energy. We refer to it as Higher Power, or Power Greater.

Today I will not judge others by how they refer to or connect with their God or Higher Power. I will concentrate on knowing my relationship with my source of strength, wisdom, love, and guidance.

◆ ◆ ◆

December 7

Recovery is self-care.
—DAVE KULSRUD

◆　◆　◆

When we get into the routine of taking care of ourselves, we notice a difference. We learn techniques that help us reduce stress levels. We get ourselves on a stress prevention program. We feel better about ourselves in general. When we start to feel tense and anxious, we know what to do, whether it be to get exercise, a massage, a hot bath, or extra sleep.

If we're doing our best to alleviate stress yet repeatedly find ourselves having to give extra time and energy to dealing with it, we look at the source of it. We look at our behavior. What are we doing, or not doing, that causes stress? Are we taking on too much work? Stuffing our bills in a drawer? Allowing "toxic" people to run our lives?

**Today I will aim to prevent,
not just medicate, stress.**

◆　◆　◆

December 8

Darkness cannot drive out darkness; only light can do that. Hate cannot drive out hate; only love can do that.

—MARTIN LUTHER KING JR.

◆ ◆ ◆

Ebenezer Scrooge was a lonely, miserable old man until the ghosts of Christmas past, present, and future showed him firsthand all he had to be grateful for. The simple act of gratitude transformed the grumpy, miserly, unbendable Scrooge into a laughing, generous, lovable soul overnight. Gratitude is that powerful; it transforms instantaneously.

An attitude of gratitude is not only powerful, it's a quick fix, and it's free. All we have to do is think of a situation that bothers us, see the little bit of good in it, and thank our Higher Power for that little piece of good. Then we go down the list. We think of every person, place, and thing that annoys us and thank our Higher Power. Before we're done, we're not only consumed with feelings of love and joy but we're also ecstatic about our lot in life. It's really not so bad, after all.

Today I will thank my Higher Power for the awareness my debt has brought me.

◆ ◆ ◆

December 9

> Forgiveness is the fragrance the violet
> sheds on the heel that has crushed it.
>
> —MARK TWAIN

◆　◆　◆

Resentment is old anger. Some resentments are a day old; others are decades old. Resentments are something we carry with us wherever we go. We're angry with someone for something he or she did or didn't do. For whatever reason, we never resolved the anger. We either never talked about it or we couldn't let go of it. When we've reached the resentment stage, it doesn't really matter who was at fault. The point is that *we're* holding on to the negative feeling. By carrying it, we pay the price, regardless of who was at fault.

Resentments can keep us from moving forward. It takes energy to carry a grudge. Releasing resentment involves forgiveness. But how do we get far enough past these hateful feelings to be able to forgive? The fastest, most effective way to let go of resentment is to pray for the people we resent. The more we resent them, the more we pray for them.

**Today I will pray for every person
I have a negative thought about.**

◆　◆　◆

December 10

Reality is the things we cannot possibly not
know, sooner or later, in one way or another.

—HENRY JAMES

♦ ♦ ♦

It's crystal clear to us why we're in debt. Our spouses
can't keep jobs or won't stop gambling or spending
compulsively. Why don't they admit that they're responsible for our debt? Why don't they admit to the truth?

Denial is strong. People use denial to protect themselves from the pain of facing a difficult reality. We can't
expect that others will see the writing on the wall if
they're in denial. Rather than beat them over the head
with the information and live with the rage we have,
we accept the truth and know that we can't force
another to do the same. We stop trying to convince others. We instead turn to meeting our basic needs; we ask
ourselves what those are.

Today I will accept a simple truth:
I cannot change others.

♦ ♦ ♦

December 11

Money is like manure. You have
to spread it around or it smells.

—J. PAUL GETTY

◆　◆　◆

We're so in debt. We can hardly pay for our groceries. How can we possibly think about giving
money to church or a charity?

When we give, willingly, we feel abundant. We feel
like we have something others can benefit from. This
makes us feel worthy, and it makes us feel rich. These
feelings alone are enough to sustain us at times. When
we give and feel abundance, it circulates in our lives.

Today I will trust that what I give I also receive.

◆　◆　◆

December 12

A gift is something that you want
but that you would not buy for yourself.

—ALBERT SIRVAITIS

◆　◆　◆

We want to give the perfect gifts, and we think we need to spend money to do it. Most people buy what they need, and it's sometimes impossible to guess what people really want—if they really want anything at all.

When we give of ourselves, we give a special gift, one that can't be bought or wrapped. We may not feel like it's much, but the recipient feels the beauty of it. They know it's easy to spend money but an effort to spend time and energy. They know you care.

Today I will look through books to find ideas for homemade gifts and other ways I can give of myself during the holidays.

◆　◆　◆

December 13

Spirituality is the quality of our relationships
with self, others, and a Higher Power.

—JOHN MAC DOUGALL

◆　◆　◆

We are all made of mind, body, and spirit. Because
spirit is impalpable, some of us have a hard time
grasping exactly what spirituality is. Our spirit is the part
of us touched by God, or our Higher Power. It's the part
of us that connects us to other people and to the rest
of the universe. It's our drive and desire. If we ignore
our spirit, we ignore who and what we are and why we
are here.

Our spirituality is how our spirit feels about how it's
conducting business. Have we been treating our business partners fairly? Were we kind to the boy who
packed our groceries? Did we call Mom this week? Do
we think we're worthy of making more money? Have
we prayed today? Meditated? Do we respect nature?

All of our actions and thoughts—with and about ourselves, others, and our Higher Power—make up how we
feel about ourselves, others, and our Higher Power. If
we have the best intentions to be good and kind to all,
our spirituality improves automatically. We feel the
goodness in return. We attract it.

**Today I will make a conscious effort to
treat myself, others, and my Higher Power
with respect and kindness.**

◆　◆　◆

December 14

He who created you without you will not justify you
without you.

—SAINT JOHN CHRYSOSTOM

◆　◆　◆

Many of us make excuses for our debt. We believe our circumstances are special; therefore, our debt is justified. We're actors, freelance writers, or real estate agents, in fields that don't have steady incomes. We've been on welfare all our lives, we never went to college, English is our second language, we have six children, we're paying child support, we're in chronic pain, our spouse is a gambler, we were laid off, or we have a criminal record.

It's true that each of us has a reason for being in debt. Instead of assuming that our case is special and there-fore it's okay for us to incur lots of unsecured debt, we accept that we are choice-making adults responsible for our behavior and for meeting our challenges. We don't have to think we're so strong we can do it alone, but we don't have to think we're so weak we can't make a positive difference in our lives.

**Today I will think of one reason
why my debt is not justifiable.**

◆　◆　◆

December 15

[Generosity] consists less in giving much
than in giving at the right moment.

—JEAN DE LA BRUYÈRE

◆ ◆ ◆

When someone is being generous to us, most of us feel all warm and fuzzy inside. It makes us feel good, special, and lucky. We're happy to know, or to stumble across, a generous person. When intentions are pure, being generous and accepting generosity are wonderful things. Everybody wins. Everybody feels good.

All of these feelings go to the wayside, however, when the intentions of either party are less than pure. If we're giving money and gifts to show off, or if we're asking for money because we're irresponsible with ours, the joy of giving and receiving is lost.

When we give or lend money to people whose intentions are good, and when we're cautious about enabling people who haven't come to grips with their money issues, we have the perfect combination of being good to others as well as to ourselves.

Today I will have pure intentions.

◆ ◆ ◆

December 16

Choice has always been a privilege
of those who could afford to pay for it.

—ELLEN FRANKFORT

◆ ◆ ◆

Most of us are drawn to spending money on certain items or in certain places. We may have a
fondness for anything from shoes, towels, and picture
frames to computers or fishing equipment. Or we get
all too comfortable when we're in a certain environment—a garage sale, a particular mall, a sewing shop,
a Christmas store, or a home improvement store. We
have a hard time resisting all the goodies. We don't
really need anything, but we go in just to look, or to
get one small item, and end up filling our basket and
emptying our pockets.

Just as an alcoholic may be wise to avoid bars,
debtors (whether compulsive spenders or not) are wise
to avoid slippery places. If we don't go to the mall, we
can't spend any money there. If we don't go to the race-
track, we can't bet on the horses.

**Today I will identify my slippery places
or items and decide how to avoid them.**

◆ ◆ ◆

December 17

> Great works are performed not
> by strength but by perseverance.
>
> —SAMUEL JOHNSON

◆　◆　◆

We have errands to run. We need to go to the grocery store, the department store, and the gas station. We know exactly what it is we need at each location. Each stop, however, is a potential dumping ground for our cash. While we're heading toward the pet section at Kmart for fish food, we're easily sidetracked by the Christmas items in aisle two.

We know we don't need any more Christmas decorations. We have enough wrapping paper. Christmas items are not on our spending plan. We have crates full of them in the basement.

Before we go into a slippery place, we bring only enough cash for what we plan to buy. We hide the money we need for our other errands in the car. We then remind ourselves of what we came in to buy. We came to get fish food—we have to have it, and we're not going to leave without it. Lastly, we tell ourselves we will not debt for this twenty-four hours.

Today I will not debt.

◆　◆　◆

December 18

The horologe of eternity
sayeth this incessantly—
"Forever—never!
Never—forever!"

—HENRY WADSWORTH LONGFELLOW

◆ ◆ ◆

We're tempted to think *once in debt, always in debt.* In our heads, it's all or nothing. It's forever. We'll always feel obligated, we'll always be behind, we'll never get ahead.

Debt is not forever. For most of us, debt, like a scraped knee, is temporary. We only need to accept that we're in debt, acknowledge how we got here, and take steps to get and stay out of debt. End of story.

Today I will have foresight.

◆ ◆ ◆

December 19

We don't have time not to have time.

—GARY BURKE

◆　◆　◆

Praying is talking to our Higher Power. Meditating is listening to our Higher Power. Various methods of meditation exist. One form is to sit, shoulders relaxed and palms up, and to focus on a word, such as "peace." The object is to clear the mind of all thoughts. For beginners, this may be difficult, but it gets easier with practice.

Once our minds are clear—once the ego is out of the picture—we feel in touch with our inner selves. We *know* what's true. Solutions to our problems just come to us. We feel a sense of calm.

Today I will meditate for ten to thirty minutes. I will make meditation part of my daily regimen.

◆　◆　◆

December 20

Any idiot can face a crisis. It's the
day-to-day living that wears you out.

—ANTON CHEKHOV

◆ ◆ ◆

When we're in a crisis, the stress response kicks in. The adrenaline starts to flow, our heart starts to pound, and we're able to move quickly—fight or flight. We have this feature for a reason. As cave dwellers, we needed to move quickly when face-to-face with a bear, for instance. We still call on the response to run from predators, to defend ourselves or loved ones in danger, or to brake in time before hitting a dog.

The problem is that many of us allow ourselves to stay at an elevated level of stress. Some of us are so accustomed to being there we don't even realize it—we think it's normal. Being stressed out almost all the time is taxing on our bodies. It wears us out! We learn to get stressed out, and we can learn how to relax. Relaxation is a skill that gets easier with practice.

Today I will practice deep breathing. I will get
into a comfortable position; slowly breathe
in through my nose and watch my abdomen rise;
slowly release my breath through my mouth.
I will concentrate only on my breathing
for at least one minute.

◆ ◆ ◆

December 21

The way your money is delivered may change radical-
ly and frequently, but the source never changes.
It is the same yesterday, today, and forever.

—MARY HUNT

❖ ❖ ❖

We think of our employers, spouses, parents, or
investments as the sources of our money. If we
lose our job, if we upset our spouse or parents, or if the
stock market drops, we think we'll be in big trouble. We
depend on our source of income. We fear that if it is
gone, we'll be in bigger financial trouble than ever.

We replace fear with faith. Instead of viewing a person, place, or thing as the source, we see our Higher
Power, the universe, as our source. God, or our Higher
Power, gave each of us talent. If we use our talent, if
we are responsible, if we honor and respect the money
we've been given access to, if we don't hoard it but are
instead giving, if we are good stewards of our money
and our lives, we will never want.

Today all my needs will be met.

❖ ❖ ❖

December 22

To dry one's eyes and laugh at a fall,
And baffled, get up and begin again.

—ROBERT BROWNING

❖   ❖   ❖

Every now and then, life brings each and every one of us a new challenge. It may be divorce, death of a loved one, illness, addiction, or debt. Whether we stumble, fall flat on our face, or get pushed over the side of a cliff, we have to meet the challenge. We have to get up again and get to the point where we can look back not with tears but with laughter.

During the fall, we are usually baffled. *Why did this happen to me?* Over time, as we grow from meeting the challenge, we understand. It's at that point that we can laugh, or at least smile, at our fall.

Today I will know that starting over is a part of everyone's life at one time or another.

❖   ❖   ❖

December 23

Great men are they who see that the spiritual is stronger than any material force, that thoughts rule the world.

—RALPH WALDO EMERSON

◆ ◆ ◆

We can waste a lot of energy trying to make things happen, complaining about what isn't working, and blaming others for our financial troubles. It's not just physical, mental, and emotional energy. Most significantly, we spend our precious spiritual energy on the negatives in our life.

We need to conserve our spiritual energy, to keep it within, and to make it grow so we can use it to create and fuel abundance. We return to the basics of our spirituality. We concentrate on practicing goodness in our relationships with ourselves, others, and our Higher Power. When we allow ourselves to focus on heightening these three basic aspects of our lives, all else falls into place. We don't even have to try. We conserve and even increase our spiritual energy.

**Today I will increase my energy
by focusing it on the basics.**

◆ ◆ ◆

December 24

A believer is one in whom persuasion and
belief had ripened into faith, and faith
became a passionate intuition.

—WILLIAM WORDSWORTH

♦   ♦   ♦

When we don't know what to do, many of us act
in haste or don't do anything at all. Either reaction can work to our benefit or demise. We're confused.
We may not even know if we're responding to a gut feeling, an intuition, a fear, or misinformation. Any action
we take is by chance.

Most decisions in life don't require an immediate
answer. Unless there's an emergency, we usually have
some time—or can ask for some time—to process. When
we don't know whether to buy or rent, file bankruptcy
or tough it out, stay together or divorce, take a new job
or accept a raise, close the business or put more money
into it, we allow ourselves time—quiet time. We pray,
we meditate, and we listen. We ask our Higher Power
for a sign of what to do next. In our connection with
our Higher Power, we discover the right answer.

Today I will pray, meditate, listen, and believe.

♦   ♦   ♦

December 25

Some people walk in the rain. Others just get wet.
—ROGER MILLER

◆　◆　◆

Gifts are usually surprises. We don't generally know what the ribbons, bows, and wrapping conceal.

Life's greatest misfortunes are, in retrospect, often referred to as gifts. While our debt can feel like a curse, when we finally get to the bottom of what's happened to us, we're surprised to find something good—a gift or blessing of sorts. Through our misfortune, we may have developed some true and lasting relationships, learned we had some admirable qualities we didn't know we had, or discovered the meaning of courage.

Today, if I am struggling, I will anticipate the wondrous surprises to come.

◆　◆　◆

December 26

To practice five things under all circumstances
constitutes perfect virtue; these five are gravity,
generosity of soul, sincerity, earnestness, and kindness.

—CONFUCIUS

◆   ◆   ◆

Some of us were raised to decline generosity—to
argue over who pays the restaurant bill, not to
accept money for helping someone out, not to accept
food or drink at someone's home. Some of these beliefs
have strong cultural ties. Others are just a fear of
imposing. We don't want to be a bother.

Generosity is a two-way street. It's just as important
for someone to be generous as it is to accept the offer-
ings. Most of us like to be generous. When we're being
genuine, from the heart, with no strings attached, being
generous makes us feel good—it makes us feel great. We
have no reason to deny others that feeling (unless, of
course, there are strings attached). In fact, our own generosity is probably just coming back to us.

**Today I will allow others the
opportunity to be generous.**

◆   ◆   ◆

December 27

The necessities were going by default to save
the luxuries until we hardly knew which were
necessities and which were luxuries.

—FRANK LLOYD WRIGHT

◆　◆　◆

How do we define necessity when we're in debt?
Many of us have blurred the distinction between
need and want. The average household owns computers, TVs, VCRs, CD players, and microwaves and has
a garage full of tools and closets jam-packed with
clothes and shoes.

We step back and review our priorities, values, and
physical, mental, spiritual, and emotional needs. How
often, for example, do we watch the movie channels on
cable TV? If we're homebound and don't get out to see
movies regularly, spending money on cable movie stations is most likely a gratifying and money-saving
expenditure. We could justify the cost as meeting a
need. If we seldom have the TV on except to watch the
news, we might be better off paying to order a movie
once a month, renting from a video store, or going to
the movie theater.

**Today I will analyze whether I'm
spending from need or from want.**

◆　◆　◆

December 28

We must select the illusion which appeals to
our temperament and embrace it with passion,
if we want to be happy.
—CYRIL CONNOLLY

◆ ◆ ◆

Most of us at some point have wanted what we can't have, or think we can't have. If we've been depriving ourselves or are underearners, we may feel guilty or—at the other extreme—overly entitled when we purchase something we want.

It's okay to want, but it's important to stop and consider whether our want aligns with our priorities and values. If it does, we revisit our spending plan. If the want is immediate, how can we manage it? Can we take a little from each category and make it happen? If it's not immediate, we add it to our spending plan and save for it.

Today I will know that real wants are achievable.

◆ ◆ ◆

December 29

Each handicap is like a hurdle in a steeplechase,
and when you ride up to it, if you throw
your heart over, the horse will go along too.

—LAWRENCE BIXBY

◆　◆　◆

Life can be overwhelming—work, children, traffic, responsibilities. Add to it debt, addiction, and other troubles, and we're in the midst of complete chaos. We have days where we can't sort through how we feel. How do we get to the root of it all if we can't even think straight?

We write about a trying situation and describe how we feel. The act of transferring our thoughts and feelings to paper relieves us of burdens, helps to clear our minds, and somehow diminishes the intense and often destructive power our thoughts can have over us. We reach a new awareness. We don't need to be great writers. We don't need to share our writings. We only need to be honest, willing, and consistent as we attempt to write daily.

Today I will find a notepad and begin writing a daily journal.

◆　◆　◆

December 30

The soul, like the moon, is new, and always new again.

—LALLESWARI

◆ ◆ ◆

Life, like the moon, has its cycles. We experience pain and growth, joy and renewal. We look back at the start of our journey and think of how far we've come. How are we different today than we were yesterday, one month ago, one year ago?

Maybe we've paid off a large chunk of debt; maybe we've hardly made a dent. But we also look at what we've done with the primary purpose in our lives—how far have we come in our relationship with ourselves, others, and our Higher Power?

We are here in part to evolve. Pain and joy equal evolution. We're moving forward, not backward. We know and trust that it's all worth it. We feel the difference.

Today I can be grateful for the newer, richer self I've chosen to develop.

◆ ◆ ◆

December 31

Words that do not match deeds are not important.

—CHE GUEVARA

◆　◆　◆

We say we want to get out of debt. We say we need more money. We say we need a higher-paying job. We say we're going to stop gambling. We say we're going to take better care of our health. We say we're going to pay someone back. We say we're going to start a spending plan. We say we're going to start recording our expenses. All of this and more we say we'll do *someday.*

With the new year approaching, we commit to doing the positive things we say we're going to do, regardless of how tiresome, boring, or painful they may be. When we really don't want to go ahead with it—whatever it may be—we remind ourselves of the commitment we made. We write it down. We fulfill our commitment. In doing so, we affirm that we really can have or do what we say. We feel better about ourselves, and others find us trustworthy and honorable. We create integrity.

**Today, on this New Year's Eve,
I will act as if my word is my law.**

◆　◆　◆

INDEX

◆ ◆ ◆

Karen Casanova graduated from college debt-free only to find herself in the throes of debt after her marriage to a compulsive gambler. After a divorce, she struggled not only to pay bills but also to find hope for the future. Spirituality and practicality became her saving graces. In *Letting Go of Debt,* Casanova shares some of the tools that help her maintain serenity while she strives for financial independence. Casanova is the author of thirteen children's books under various pen names. She has worked as an editor for the past fifteen years. Originally from Dearborn, Michigan, she now resides in Saint Croix Falls, Wisconsin.

About Hazelden Publishing

As part of the Hazelden Betty Ford Foundation, Hazelden Publishing offers both cutting-edge educational resources and inspirational books. Our print and digital works help guide individuals in treatment and recovery, and their loved ones. Professionals who work to prevent and treat addiction also turn to Hazelden Publishing for evidence-based curricula, digital content solutions, and videos for use in schools, treatment programs, correctional programs, and electronic health records systems. We also offer training for implementation of our curricula.

Through published and digital works, Hazelden Publishing extends the reach of healing and hope to individuals, families, and communities affected by addiction and related issues.

For more information about Hazelden publications, please call **800-328-9000** or visit us online at **hazelden.org/bookstore**.